THINK
FEEL
SING

A CLEAR PATH TO EASY SINGING

A Portrait of the Artist as a Young Man

THINK
FEEL
SING

A CLEAR PATH TO EASY SINGING

Franco Spoto

Dunham Road Productions, Publisher

Copyright © 2017, Franco Spoto

THIRD EDITION

© 2017 By Franco Spoto

All rights reserved. This book or any portion thereof may not be reproduced or used in any manner whatsoever without the express written permission of the publisher, except for the use of brief quotations in a book review or scholarly journal.

ISBNs:
978-1-62217-524-6 (hardback)
978-1-62217-383-9 (paperback, 1st edition)
978-1-5356-0060-6 (paperback, 2nd edition)
978-1-5356-0794-0 (paperback, 3rd edition)
978-1-62217-384-6 (epub)
978-1-62217-385-3 (mobi)

Drawing, Figure 3 by Betti Franceschi
Figures 4-18 by Franco Spoto
Photographs: Frontispiece by Chuck Karel; p. 23 by Andrew Eskind[2] ; p. 39 by Franco Spoto
Cover design by Franco Spoto

Published by
Dunham Road Productions
77 Dunham Road
East Chatham, NY 12060 USA

In memory of Richard L. Thompson (1925 - 2014), who, as a teacher, by example and mentoring, inspired and encouraged love and respect for all styles of music from Palestrina to Bernstein and for all of life. Commitment and perseverance learned in his presence have brought me through the long journey to the understanding that I offer in this book.

ACKNOWLEDGMENTS

I am grateful for every teacher who welcomed me into the studio, for every student who has come to me to learn and for the opportunity to work with a remarkable group of people at Belvoir Terrace in Lenox, MA. In teaching it is I who learned so much about our wonderful gifts. Specific to this book's evolution I thank Solomon Epstein and Barbara Martin Green for detailed and insightful analysis of the text and intent of the book and for general editorial suggestions. So important to the task have been Mary Deyerle Hack for depth of perspective, encouragement and careful analysis, Jacqueline Presti for probing questions, and Michael D. Roberts for a broad range of skills and ideas brought to many readings as I sought to clarify the difficult expression of feelings in the mind-body weave that is our nature. I sing praises of my editor, Elizabeth Guinn Miller, a skilled professional whose love for this subject and belief in this presentation of it afforded me so much support.

Not least, I am deeply grateful to my wife, Dianne, a very patient woman who has always given me the space and time to become and to express myself.

Finally, I give thanks to T.S. Eliot who nailed the essence of self-discovery and awareness in these lines:

"We shall not cease from exploration,
and the end of all our exploring will be to arrive where we started and know the place for the first time."

Contents

Acknowledgements vi
Preface to the Second Edition 1
Preface to the First Edition 5
Introduction..9
The Bigger Picture 15
Mind Your Voice! 17
The Body and the Law 23
Terms and Images...27
The Jaw...35
Keep on Hummin' 39
The Breath When Singing 45
Phonation 53
Tone Columns 57
Awareness Exercises...61
Vowel Modification 71
Tuning the Instrument..73
Momentum 77
In Summary 85

Appendices

Appendix A: A Contemplation 89
Appendix B: Hand Jive for Singers 93
Appendix C: Frequently Asked Questions...............................97
Appendix D: Seven Pillars of Vocal Wisdom 105

Appendix E: 26 Exercises 107
About the Exercises 115
Glossary..121
Recommended Reading 123
Notes 125
About the Author 127

PREFACE TO THE SECOND EDITION

SPECIFIC ACTIONS MUST OCCUR WITHIN a flexible structure in order to sing optimally; i.e., with accurate musical response to concepts of tone and phrasing, with desired resonance and colors and no unwanted tension. This is true for all styles of music.

How does that happen? There is a small mountain of literature about the science of the voice today with anatomical analysis of parts and physiology, voice prints and so many other measuring modalities to show us how things should be as we search for what must have been known by at least a few master teachers 150 years ago. Garcia, Lehmann, Hislop, Cotogni, Lamperti, Herbert-Caesari and many others carefully shaped the physical, mental and emotional bodies of some of the world's greatest singing artists. There are always great voices, but in the past 100 years the number of great singers has dwindled with every decade. Why?

Searching for what seems to have been lost, I am reminded of a famous true story entitled: Acres of Diamonds.

A farmer in South Africa despaired of becoming wealthy in the very country of diamonds. He sold his farm and traveled the continent in search of the precious stones until he had spent all his resources, gave up hope and drowned himself in a river. Meanwhile, the man who had bought his farm picked up an unusual rock one day, and upon examination by a friend, discovered it to be one of the largest diamonds ever found. In fact the entire farm was littered with these rocks. We know that farm today as the Kimberly Diamond Mine, simply the richest in the world. Wealth had been under his feet for the taking, but unnoticed, he looked for answers "out there".

Over the kitchen entrance of a luncheonette near my home there is a sign which reads: Go within or go without. Cute, since the food is within, but what does this have to do with singing, which is a giving out, not a looking in?

When you pour liquid into a vessel it has to come from a source, a pitcher, a bottle. So what is the source of the "giving out" when you sing? Where does your voice originate? Your voice is born of your imagination. That seems obvious but, in my experience, it is not considered carefully enough while developing your senses of singing. Your imagination is not only the source of emotion and the style of your music, but of the playing of you, the instrument.

My mother's younger sister was a concert pianist of some stature early in her career in Canada. A protégé of Bartok, she studied with him in Hungary where he would stuff the piano with quilts so that her only sense of sound came through her finger tips; total dependence upon physical sensation and her imagination's concept of the sound. When she related that story to me, I was moved, but not until I understood myself as a singing instrument did I grasp its life-changing implications.

When you hear the sound you intend within your mind as though it were resounding in your head in the best quality that you can conceive, you can notice feelings throughout your body. Those feelings are your subconscious mind showing you exactly what those sounds feel like; exactly what you, the instrument feels and looks like. Learning to trust your feelings can open a window to self-awareness and mastery that will change forever your joy of singing.

All that you will ever need to know in order to enjoy your very own acres of diamonds is already within you. Allow me to show you the difference between an interesting rock and a precious diamond.

Franco Spoto, May, 2016

PREFACE TO THE FIRST EDITION

BEGINNING IN AUGUST 1997, AND for five years, I was a voice instructor in a one-week-long music camp for extraordinary people at Belvoir Terrace, an estate in Lenox, MA. Engaged to teach, to guide, to coach, I found myself more the student. My goal was to help them find joy in the feelings of singing. By example, they opened me to new appreciation of the feelings of living. In my view, life is. Some, as I, might argue that life is all there is. Living is how you embrace life.

The campers were diagnosed with Williams Syndrome, a condition identified in 1961 by a cardiologist in New Zealand, J. C. P. Williams. First considered to be an anomaly of the aorta, in 1993 further analysis showed, additionally, a deletion of a varying number of genes from what is seen as the long arm of one of the 29 pairs of human chromosomes. That latter aspect of its nature accounts for a variety of manifest symptoms in those with WS. In general, Attention Deficit Disorder and varying motor and spatial recognition shortfalls are balanced by unusual gregariousness, verbal skills and musical senses bordering on savant. One of my students frequently extemporized a song at the piano based on the first few sentences that we exchanged in the lesson.

During one particular session, a student began a simple five-note scale. After the fourth note he was unable to continue, seemingly tone-deaf to the pitch of the fifth note, one easily within his vocal range. He had lost his concentration and seemed unwilling or unable to regain it. In an effort to keep the experience positive, I suggested that he not try to sing the pitch out loud, but rather play it on a piano in his head, in his imagination. I played the note on the piano in the studio and asked, "Can you play that note on the piano in your head?" He replied that he was doing that. I asked, "What does it sound like?" and he sang the note accurately with no scooping from below or above, as though he had opened a window allowing us to hear the pitch already resonating within.

"Think ahead!" had been a direction from every teacher I had known and it did help when implemented, but something was missing. I re-examined every aspect of vocal technique that I had found useful along the decades of studying, performing, teaching. There was no silencing the questions that echoed in my mind: What if thinking ahead by itself had little to do within the art of singing without taking the time to feel the body's responses to the thoughts? What if, when feeling those responses, I could learn to see the body at work as a definitive vocal instrument? What if allowing or releasing the sound through the imagined instrument, as though singing in my head and letting you hear it, was the only surely accurate, foolproof way to "play"the voice? Really? Could it be that simple? Could so complex a coordination be so easily understood? This is how impersonators do what they do. They mimic details of body language as well. Why not impersonate the best image of ourselves in the style of singing that gives us the most joy? Granted, the elements of the living, breathing, functioning voice would have to be balanced and strengthened where needed, but it's that coordination which confounds so many. This was one dramatic course correction; only a couple of degrees but an enormous difference in the end.

Since that refreshing epiphany, my life has been dedicated to awareness of the structure, the moving parts within it and exercises which can make the desired results inevitable; all in the context of learning from my imagination as teacher. There have been so many "aha!" moments, feeling and recognizing sensations suggested/demanded one way or another by teachers I had known, but which I had not fully understood, seen, felt. To be sure, the coordination of all the parts of the singing body is complex, but we who are not naturals confuse our quest for ease when we ignore what our perfect imaginations show us.

Originally written for my students as a reference to help with their work between lessons, this book was read by a few others whose opinions I highly value. They have encouraged me to make the project widely available.

We no longer enjoy the 19th-century practice of auditioning for a master teacher and, upon acceptance into the studio, studying one or two hours a day, six days a week for four to six years until singing was mastered. The student did not dare sing anywhere in public during the years of development; not an "Ave Maria" in church or a chorus of "O Sole Mio" at a party. Would an artist exhibit an unfinished canvas?

I intentionally avoid explaining what is less than constructive about much vocal teaching today. Believing that whatever is in your crosshairs becomes your target, I ignore the periphery. There are no shortcuts to master so complex a coordination as singing, but it is not difficult to understand when the path of truth is well-lit. Like the proverbial journey of a thousand miles, you begin with the first step and continue through each succeeding pace until the end is under your feet. Keep your eyes on the road, but your mind on the destination.

You will find here much repetition of basics in various contexts because there is only one lesson, usually requiring many viewpoints until perspective is obtained and, like the figure hidden in the marbled rectangle on the comics page in Sunday papers, obscurity changes to clarity. The goal is to learn three overriding aspects of "natural" artistic singing in any style: 1) the structure and carriage of the vocal body, head to hips; 2) the movements of the various elements of the vocal apparatus in response to thoughts of vowels, pitches and colors; and 3) your imagination's playing of the balanced instrument. That's Rome: many roads leading there, but only one Rome.

It is not enough to describe a feeling to a student. There must be presented and demonstrated exercises which make the feeling inevitable. The exercises and images are designed to build awareness of the structure of the vocal body and habits of coordination — muscle memories — which serve to help you respond accurately and musically to your sense of the composition, allowing you to reach the singer's intention: clear, emotional communication.

Above all, know that these are tools. Once you understand yourself as a physical instrument in balance, strength and flexibility, simply enjoy the feelings, see the whole picture and allow your musical senses to flow. Put the tools away until a repair may be necessary. Then thank all that's holy that you have the understanding and means to deal with an emergency. Bathe yourself in resonance and color. It's good for you at every level of your existence.

Franco Spoto, July 2015, East Chatham, NY

INTRODUCTION

I DON'T BELIEVE THAT ONE can learn singing from books; stimulate, corroborate ideas, clarify images, perhaps, but learning's best achieved under the guidance of a knowledgeable instructor and continuing analysis of what one feels. This book should be read as adjunct to private study. I draw upon decades of performing, of curiosity and research, listening to great singers, reading, and most importantly, feeling the elements of my own voice. I am the body of evidence.

My journey began as a young teenager listening to recordings and seeing the movies of Mario Lanza. Naïve to any technical shortcomings in his singing, I was enthralled by the sound of his voice, as was the better part of the rest of the world. Then I was introduced to Jussi Björling, Tito Schipa, Frank Sinatra, Ella Fitzgerald, Renata Tebaldi. With such varied colors, styles and dynamics, they all shared one unmistakable factor: mastery. The ease with which their voices poured from them as though the sounds were beams of light led me to ask: How can a human voice do that?

Apparently (that is, my parents told me) I had been singing since I was a toddler, then as a soprano in church choirs and a tenor in high school vocal ensembles, leading to my answering an ad for a soloist position at the Congregational Church in Teaneck, NJ at the age of 16. A generous and kindly organist/choir director named Nelson Doescher gave me extra credit for chutzpah (read: naïveté) and offered me the "second tenor" spot. I was on my way to answering the burning question: "How?" The first tenor soloist was Rod MacWherter, soon to be a Wagnerian tenor at the Met. The bass was a gentle giant named Paul Plishka, who would go on to be one of the mainstays at the Met in bass repertoire for decades.

In this company, I thought that I should begin to understand what I was doing (to that point by sheer dint of will). I soon learned of an old-school teacher in New York City, Mario Fiorella. I took a bus into the city at the George Washington Bridge and subways downtown to 853 Seventh Avenue from our home in New Milford, NJ twice a week after school, paying for the lessons with savings from my paper route and help from my parents. The path was chosen. An audition and early acceptance at The Oberlin College Conservatory of Music grounded me securely.

Four years later and fresh out of Oberlin, I began my professional life as an instructor of singing, music theory, and conducting at Bluffton College, now Bluffton University, in western Ohio. It was a stable start and one which I happily might have continued, were it not for my driving quest to understand more deeply the truths of vocal mechanics and their relationship to artistry in performance.

I have to imagine that all singing teachers mean well, but some are informed more wisely than others. In my opinion, the instructor must have a disciplinary knowledge of the physical vocal instrument and techniques of its functions which can lead to the art of singing: a knowledge based on textbook physiology combined with experience in self-development and performance. The instructor must be able to articulate in various phrases and images the efforts that make the desired results inevitable. One student may understand one description while another needs to see/feel it another way.

While Mario Fiorella had a rich and beautiful voice, had been a successful baritone at the Chicago Lyric and elsewhere, had learned to sing in the studio of Mario Sammarco and was capable of hurting none, it was my last teacher, James Carson, who introduced me to myself as a physical instrument. He was the first to show how specific exercises could make desired results inevitable. He studied at some point in London with Alma Caesari, superb singer, daughter and pupil of E. Herbert-Caesari. Herbert-Caesari had been a student of Riccardo Daviesi in Italy. Daviesi, a master teacher, had been one of the last and greatest of the Sistine Chapel Singers. While all instructors helped me see things previously unnoticed, the line descending from Daviesi through Carson most permeates my understanding of the singer's instrument and art.

Given all the vocal sounds that we can emit, I concern myself here with communicative singing, the blending of words, rhythm and melody: one of the most natural expressions of the human condition. Regardless of the cruel, unthinking taunts of acquaintances, family and even some "teachers" who declare that an individual cannot sing, virtually anyone, even the so-called tone-deaf, can sing with a little guidance and understanding. I will speak to this statement in greater detail in the section headed "Mind Your Voice!"

We were born to sing. Babies sing before they speak. Our voices are uniquely melodic, while speech is like using only low gears in a Ferrari. Rev it up and let go. Singing is overdrive for your spirit. People who believe that singing is beyond their ability can be heard quietly humming or singing when unaware that there might be someone listening. Those who confidently enjoy singing, find themselves in a variety of choral organizations, barbershop quartets, open-mic night at karaoke bars and on up to front and center onstage in rock, pop, religious, operatic, musical theater, folk and jazz venues.

What can cause trouble for us is the "wee small voice within." Our words, spoken or not, have enormous power to affect our lives. A phrase which may or may not be true but which, when repeated often enough, becomes an accepted truth, is called a meme ("I can't sing" and "I can't hold a tune in a basket" are two such phrases). Memes can be inhibitors, limiters. Let them go. Change your tune to "I can sing!" and go about making it your truth.

If you knew how to release/produce sounds that you enjoyed feeling and others enjoyed hearing, what would that do for your self-confidence? Singing is not about being a star unless you want it to be. One thing that is certain is that singing is an inherent part of your nature, an expression of your consciousness, an emotional release, a tonic for your psyche, the primal scream gone pretty.

The journey to discover your melodic nature can be rested whenever you like. That you work out in a gym does not imply that you dream of a Mr. Universe crown. There are so many plateaus after becoming "fit." Hang out where you are most comfortable. The workouts that I propose here, after basic understanding of so-called support, breath pressure and sensations of resonance, can help you become the most natural pop, jazz or folk singer. The more diligently you work, the more balanced, flexible and strong your voice will become and, given those properties uniquely your own, the wider the choices of music opened to you.

An interesting corollary to this work is that the more your singing seems effortless, the more people will believe that you were born with your ability. Well, you were born with that potential, just as you were born with all your muscles. They don't see the hours of effort spent in learning to understand and shape your vocal body even before learning how to "play" it. They can't see the innate talent pent up inside an unbalanced form, now balanced and free to express itself. Singing appears effortless only when all elements are working in oil-smooth coordination so that no one piece has to compensate for another. Smile and be grateful for praise. Change your beliefs to support your dreams, removing any limits from your imagination.

> SINGING IS OVERDRIVE
> FOR YOUR SPIRIT,
> AEROBICS FOR YOUR SOUL,
> NATURE'S GIFT TO YOU.

THE BIGGER PICTURE

"*THE DRAMA OF LIFE IS a psychological one in which all the conditions, circumstances and events of your life are brought to pass by your assumptions.*"[1] What Neville (Goddard) means by the word "assumptions" is embracing the feeling of the wish fulfilled. We experience feelings in our hearts, which become sensations throughout our bodies. The thought/image/vision alone of the desire is not enough to bring it to our physical reality. In order to live your desire you must align with it energetically, emotionally, with the state of being that becomes a constant assumption. You must know it "by heart" and feel it everywhere. This is play-acting to some, but the truth of creation to those who understand and employ it.

I take the quote from Neville with permission and paraphrase it to read: *The drama of singing is a psychological one in which all the conditions, circumstances and events of your music are brought to pass by your assumptions - being the product of your understanding/feeling yourself as a physical instrument apart from your mind, played by your imagination.* Your musical thinking is focused singularly on you, the melodic instrument, as a violinist's is on the violin. There is no space in your consciousness for other thoughts. You assume the feeling of the musician, the player. Your consciousness is making music; your body is the vehicle, the instrument.

Put another way, physically singing comes through the mouth, but energetically it comes from the heart. The former is functional and can be learned. The latter is emotional, the source of feeling, of excitement, the product of imagination; in the end, the difference between a competent professional and a charismatic star. That said, everything is interconnected.

Keep in mind that building the responsive instrument, the Stradivarius that is you, is the goal, but one which by itself cannot guarantee a singing career. To sing anything is to release a flow of melody with or without words in a communication, the product of an equation that involves all of you, mind, body, and spirit. You can be guided to it but it cannot be given to you. The good news is that whether you sing only for yourself or for the public at any level, singing is creation, a state of high consciousness.

The images, exercises and contemplations that I present are intended to lead inevitably to understanding by repetition, through feeling and clarity of vision, the movements of the various parts of you, the melodic instrument. Through growing awareness, many myths will be dispelled, the joy of singing experienced, and with it a state of well-being. One thing is certain: singing is a release that you allow, not a force that you project.

> The difference between apprehension and confidence is information, which eliminates guessing about how you will sing a note, a phrase, a piece, or hoping that your voice will be there for you.

MIND YOUR VOICE!

IF YOU WOULD LIKE TO learn to play any musical instrument, you find one already built, complete with all the parts in balance, made with the proper materials necessary for playing and producing the expected sounds. Depending upon budget and seriousness of intention, the cost will vary, but the basic instrument will be in/under your hands ready to be played. Each of us has all the parts we need to be a complete instrument, but most of us bring to singing a body of varying imbalances which inhibit easy singing.

Starting at home, the admonition usually voiced at a high-decibel level: "Inside voice, please!" begins the impositions we place on our voices. Other factors can negatively affect our sound as we mature, including but not limited to whining, crying, yelling (in cheering or anger), whispering, apprehension, medical conditions like allergies, acid reflux; the list is long. Our native languages with various consonant combinations and vowel sounds play a role as well. Speech patterns, linguistically and psychologically colored, build habits into the coordination of the vocal apparatus. Is it any wonder that Italy, whose language contains pure vowels and whose words almost always end in one of those vowels, yields so many beautiful voices?

Another consideration is that voices unerringly reflect the physical, mental and emotional states of their owners at any given moment. Even a completely natural singer, one whose voice can produce any imagined tone in any style seemingly without effort, might sound constricted under stress. Understanding that resonance and color, the attractive factors in vocal tone, are products of vibration, and that optimum vibration is only possible in an environment of maximum freedom, we must strive to be stress-free and balanced, without which states there cannot be complete freedom.

Being the only musicians who are both instrument and player, we need to develop respect for the difference. The basic premise of this work is that the human voice is a physical melodic instrument, governed by laws of nature and played by the imagination.

The muscles used and their coordination are the same whether you are singing country, rock, pop, jazz, folk, musical theater or opera. The great trumpeter Wynton Marsalis uses the same horn for jazz in New Orleans and Hummel with the New York Philharmonic. Benny Goodman used the same clarinet for big band and Mozart. Provided that a completely and accurately functioning vocal instrument is understood physically, the style of musical interpretation is a product of imagination. If you can conceive the tones and phrasing of a style and your voice is balanced and strong enough with the expected timbre for that style, you can sing it successfully.

Therefore, learning the art of singing in any style begins with understanding ourselves as instruments, trained properly through mindful physical exercises. Sensations of our vocal bodies are brought to balance, made flexible, strong and responsive to the intention to produce whatever vocalism is demanded by the musical score. In this process we feel physical movements, but *the builder is thought* generating the physical response.

I cannot emphasize enough the fact that all form and action must be conceived mentally first. The physical response to the thought of a pitch, vowel and color is your subconscious awareness showing you exactly what that tone feels like. Allow it to be. Release tone through the observed feelings. Direct physical effort almost always will be inaccurate, leading to tension where it does not belong. This fact is remarkably simple but one of the most difficult aspects of singing to grasp, because ingrained in us is the concept that "I can do it!" which implies a physical effort.

There are multiple levels of consciousness at work when we sing. I have not read, heard or imagined a way to jump right in and see them all at once in the early stages of understanding. It is best to approach each level as a separate element of the singing body/awareness, exercise it mindfully until it becomes habit and then relegate it to a functional state in turn.

There is consciousness of our shells - our body in the environment and our carriage of that body. Within that carriage there is consciousness of the structure of ourselves as instruments; another of the parts of that instrument and how they move; another of the reflections, i.e. resonance, and an overall consciousness of playing the instrument as though it were a horn. In the end your will to sing alone sets into motion all elements of the balanced, strong instrument and singing becomes as easy (but never quite the same) as speaking. The physical effort of "trying" to sing directly leads to force, whereas the mental image of playing yourself as an instrument employs the power of imagination. In my opinion, power trumps force and one must know the difference. Imagination is creation. Force is manipulation, the unnatural egoistic imposition of desire, which leads to incapacitating tension.

Dr. Maxwell Maltz, in his foundational work,

Psycho-Cybernetics, published in 1960 by Simon & Schuster, presents in the most scientific context the fact that the subconscious mind does not distinguish between physical experience and an image held vividly in mind. The operative word in the previous sentence is "vividly," implying feeling as though you were living the experience in that moment. What does it *feel* like when the thought/image is held in mind? Does it remind you of Neville's proposal in the previous section, "The Bigger Picture"? The implications and applications of this knowledge have become the basis of much self-help teaching. What your imagination sees, your body instantly, if subtly, creates. With repetition it gains strength and becomes form and habit.

When conscious of your body as an instrument separate from your mind and familiar with the constantly-shifting elements within the instrument, it is crucial to literally see through yourself from behind and slightly above. You are focusing on the action of singing with your mind's eye, looking through, not with the eyes on your face. At that point whatever is before you will be seen, but will be slightly out of focus. Ever look at the marbled rectangle on the comics page of a Sunday paper? Looks like nothing known until you alter your consciousness and, with your mind's eye, behold the dragon or carriage or whatever is within. What I describe is very similar.

The longer you hold your attention on the action the more you will see. Look up at the stars on a clear night. Maintain your gaze and soon you will see so many more stars. Where were they when you first glanced up? In this work you will see many aspects of yourself, previously unnoticed, immediately. Then over time, even years, if you remain diligent in your search for your melodic self, you will see more and more, usually unable to imagine how you had missed the "new" feelings.

The exercises and contemplations presented ahead help you to envision a working model of you as a melodic vocal body. For now, know that you are the teacher, and I am the guide on the sight-seeing tour. Don't imagine that your ego knows how to move this, that or the other thing. Don't judge yourself based on your sound, but rather feel what seems easy and comfortable. Doing the exercises, mindful of what you are feeling, develops clear senses, visually and kinesthetically, of the functioning vocal body. In time, the thought of a note or phrase will engender a clearly seen and felt sense of it, even with your mouth closed. Your thoughts effectively coordinate your muscles, making clear the sensations which will soon become the general feelings of singing.

As you learn to work this way, you will become conscious of habits which do not serve you well. Ignore them. Nothing is good or bad. Either something works for your benefit or it doesn't. You give strength to anything that you think about, so pay attention ONLY to what works, is positive and builds helpful habits. Old unwanted muscle memories will atrophy and disappear from your consciousness.

THE BODY AND THE LAW

Photo by Andrew Eskind[2]

THE "OLD ITALIAN SCHOOL," THE source of the much–used and sometimes abused term "bel canto," studied the sensations of innately perfect singers and the physiology of their throats, heads and ribcages in relation to muscles throughout the body in order to understand the correlation between actions and the sensations that they generate. The result was vocal technique which followed the laws of nature, a coordination which appeared to be, because it was, perfectly natural.

What moves, how does it move, what does that movement feel like and how does it sound? None of what we understand about the mechanical functions of our voices is invented. Rather, all has been back-engineered from conversations with "born" singers whose sensations were studied in order to reveal anatomical and physiological truths. Obviously laws of nature were being observed.

Oh, those laws of nature! Take a look at the strings of a piano. The lowest pitches are made by the longest, thickest and relatively loosest strings. As the pitches rise up the octaves, the strings become shorter, thinner and tighter. The vocal cords are actually two ligaments attached at the front and open at the back when breathing. The front of them is attached just below the median line of the thyroid cartilage, the top of which you see and feel as your "Adam's apple." The back of the cords is attached to the top of the trachea, your windpipe, through the agency of two arytenoid cartilage "horns" on what's called the cricoid cartilage. Science likes to equate appearance to familiar images, hence horns. Provided that there is balance among the 60-odd muscles that make up the larynx and suspensory system of the neck, the cricoid cartilage is pulled up and back rather dramatically and the thyroid cartilage leans gently forward and down automatically with the thought of phonation, whether spoken or sung. Because the action is automatic, it must be allowed to occur.

In order to produce increasingly higher frequencies in obedience to the law, the vocal cords must be stretched thin, which makes them tighter. Simultaneously, they must be adducted (approximated; as close together as possible without being slammed shut). Then muscles of the larynx can automatically reduce the opening of the cords from back to front, which the *thought* of pitch commands. I repeat that all this is allowed as response to thought and obeys the same physical laws as the strings of a piano or harp: there must be a proportionately shorter, thinner and tighter element to produce higher pitch frequencies. Check out the drawings of these actions on plate 73 in Dr. Frank Netter's Atlas of Human Anatomy[3]. Also, for explanation of the physiology of these parts, pages 113 and 114 in the fourth edition of Willard R. Zemlin's Speech and Hearing Science[4] are an important source.

While pitch problems with singers are always the result of maladjustments of the vocal cords, the causes of those maladjustments vary. I could explore the many ways that we obstruct the path to freedom, to allowing proper function of the vocal cords, but observing causes only strengthens them. Learning is obtained by focusing on what you seek as though already achieved and through appropriate thoughts and actions which make their achievement inevitable. Let's look at the positive.

"I'd rather learn from one bird how to sing than teach ten thousand stars how not to dance."[5]

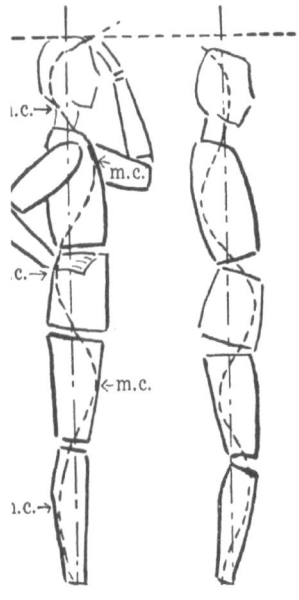 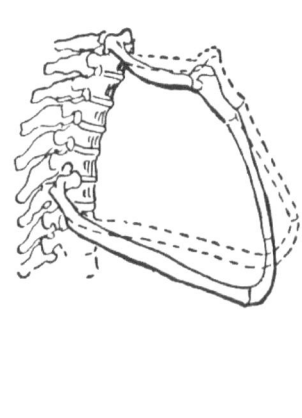

Fig. 1 Fig. 2

TERMS AND IMAGES

"You hold yourself like this.
You hold yourself like that.
By hook or crook you try to look both angular and flat."

(W. S. Gilbert, Patience)

I MISTRUST THE TERM "POSTURE" as it implies holding or placing the body in some specific attitude - chest high, shoulders back, etc. Let's agree to use the term, *carriage*. Figures 1 and 2 are found in The Thinking Body[6] by Mabel Ellsworth Todd. For more than 100 years the book has been an important study and reference in the libraries of dancers. The initials in Figure 1 stand for "muscle center." Note the centering lines and the relationship between the muscle centers on the left and on the right. The left is in balance; the right is not. Tension results from imbalance and is all-pervasive, leading to general tightness and specifically the inability to control your sound, the timbre, dynamic and flow of your music.

In Figure 2 the solid lines represent the misaligned form and the dotted, the properly aligned. With the forward and upward position of the ribcage there is more room for the lungs to expand and vital forces to flow freely, positively affecting our singing as well as general health. Seeing and holding in mind creates your reality. Physically muscling it up will only initiate unwanted tensions.

The crown of the sternum and the seventh cervical vertebra form the front and back, respectively, of the top ring of the ribcage. Imagine the entire ring as being parallel to the floor. How does that thought affect your carriage? Hold this image in mind whenever you think of it. I like to see it when walking.

While standing, ask yourself: "How long is my spine?" Feel your body's response. Then ask: "Is my skull balanced on my spine?" Don't intentionally move or hold any parts of you. Contemplate the thoughts and **observe** the physical responses, all the while asking yourself: "What does this feel like?"

One of the single most immediately effective images for understanding the poise of your carriage is that of a flexible band or arc of energy extending from inside the top back of your skull at the flat spot, the posterior fontanelle, to the coccyx or tail bone. Imagine it as an arc that can open but never crunch or close. (Figure 3) Feel it with an imagined energy lifting strongly up and back at the top, giving "lift" to the head, and down and back at the bottom, grounding itself firmly into the back of the pelvic diaphragm.

Fig. 3 A flexible arc, imagined as shown, between the back of the head and the coccyx or tail bone, connecting into the pelvic diaphragm; an IMAGINED connection. This is the center pole of a tent, without which all other senses are compromised.

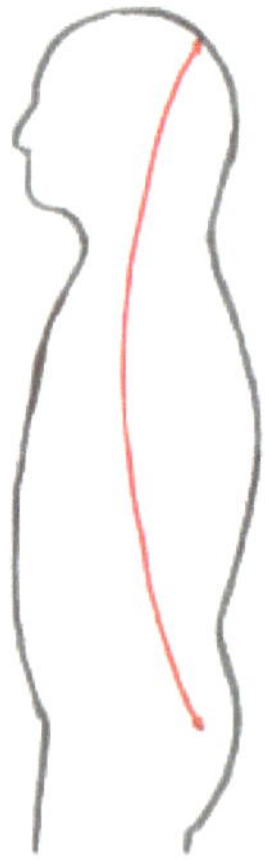

Singing: Nature's Gift To You | 29

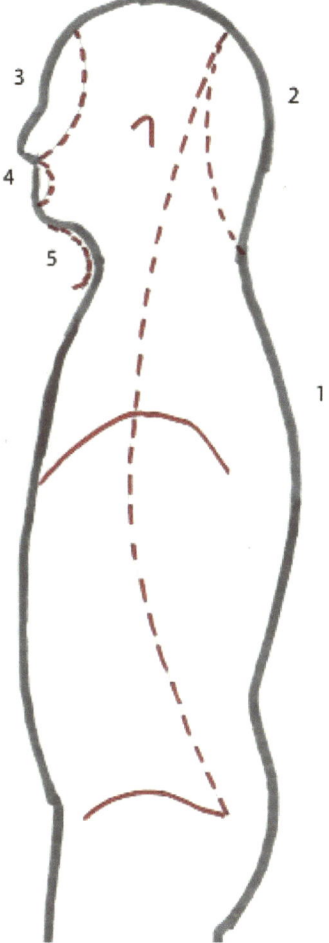

Fig. 4 "Arc-Angels" as seen in relation to the pelvic and thoracic diaphragms and to the soft palate.

I find that a system of imagined arcs lends balance and freedom to our overall sense of ourselves as functioning melodic instruments. When contemplated over time, any one of the arcs can generate a sense of the entire system, a feeling of the entire instrument. I show them in Figure 4 as I feel them. Like angels, they exist to guide us in better directions.

Number 1 is the long arc, which gives length to the spine and lift to the head. Number 2 is a shorter arc descending from the same spot as the first but inserting into the 7th cervical vertebra, yielding a more emphatic sense of lift to the head. Number 3 extends from the hairline (imagined if baldness is a condition) to immediately under the nose. Arc 3 inspires a sense of connection of the entire singing body and system of arcs. Next is an arc (4) between the bottom of the nose extending to an area just under the teeth and above the chin bone, giving a sense of having a concave shape to that area of the face. The result is a better opening of the mouth/jaw and a forward urgency, without tension, to the mandible (the lower jaw).

Finally, an arc imagined between the underside of the chin and the crown of the sternum (5) gives you the sense of wearing a neck brace. Maintaining an open feeling at that arc can prevent compression of the larynx and relieve any tension around the hyoid or tongue bone. I repeat that all these arcs should be perceived as flexible and extendible, never contracting, never closing even a little bit. The mouth arc (4) should feel as though constantly expanding in the most minute increments throughout singing, even when sustaining a note or descending in pitch.

Another term that gives me pause is "relax". Thinking while singing is a constant action inducing a constant motion, however subtle, throughout the body in response to the thoughts. A better word for the state of the singing body physical is *poised*. Poise is a condition of balanced readiness, one in which the body can allow nature to have its way. So important is the fact that we can achieve poise with imagination.

A contemplation: Imagine yourself being hollow from head to hips, an inflation so that there is equal presence on every point. With closed eyes and calm breathing, "see" your expansive hollowness. Now add the long arc to your consciousness, then the shorter (2), and each of the other arcs in turn. See/feel the skull balanced on top of the long spine. Feeling will follow seeing. Contemplate these arcs one at a time as electric, flowing energy that is never static. On a given day, add an arc to your concept of yourself as an inflation from hips up. Sing exercises and whatever music you are rehearsing with the "arc-of-the-day" in your awareness. It won't be long before you see your entire carriage as strong, balanced, flexible, and poised.

Another contemplation: Open your mouth as though yawning, which creates a very strong upward expansion in the middle of your head, balanced by a strong forward energy in the jaw. Maintaining that expansion and energy, mentally and slowly repeat vowels one after another, observing what moves and how. Soon you will see how everything, head to hips, interconnects in a seamless fabric of energies. Always ask questions, feel, experiment, and see yourself from behind as you search for your own voice, your own most resonant and colorful sound, trusting your imagination.

If left to conscious estimation of effort, the coordination of all the parts that move, brace or in any way "support" the emission of sound would be inaccurate among all except the most rare natural singers. Of course, what makes them "natural singers" is the fact that they are not conscious of "doing" anything. The object of the images of parts, their actions and substance where we know they can't exist, is that those **thoughts generate the forms and functions** that work best in coordinating tension-free and therefore resonant-full singing.

A common complaint is that in yielding to thought-generated actions, the singer doesn't feel in control. On the contrary, you won't feel control and the flow of singing until you abandon intentional physical effort and release your body to your imagination.

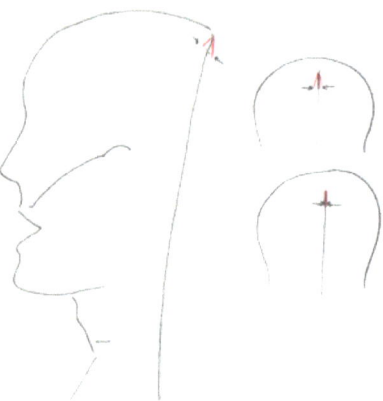

Fig. 5 An adduction IMAGE, which, when maintained has the effect of approximating the vocal cords and lifting the cricoid cartilage up and back, while urging the thyroid cartilage forward and down.

Get into the habit of taking and accepting small steps early on. It is very difficult for most people to allow physical response to thought. It requires persistent contemplation. I understand contemplation to be sustained attention. Take the time now and you will build an instrument of life-long pleasure to serve your imagination's creative flights of musical fancy.

Seeing and maintaining what I call the adduction image (Figure 5) in the upper back center of your head can engender a balanced expansive response throughout your body. Begin with the imagined arc from the upper back of your head to your tailbone. Your mouth can be open or closed. If open, it should be in a yawn-like vertical stretch. Imagine the sides of a narrow triangle at the top of the arc. Close them. Make no physical attempt to bring anything together. What do you feel everywhere when the triangle is closed? Check out one area at a time from the top of your head to your hips. Open your awareness to subtle sensations. Contemplate that as often as you can until it becomes muscle memory and jumps into place at the thought of phonation, even when speaking.

The "I can do it!" you might try to make something come together. The imaginative you will simply see it happen and know that it is so. The physical responses to this thought, some subtle, others not so, occur from the top of your skull to your pelvis. The longer you observe, the more clearly you will see/feel.

HINTS FROM THE UNIVERSE

EXPANSION GOOD but CONTRACTION BAD
FLOW GOOD, ALLOWING LIFE
STATIC BAD, FOSTERING DEATH
RESONANCE GOOD, GENERATING POWER
FORCE BAD, CREATING TENSION

THE JAW

THE MOVEMENT OF THE JAW when the mouth opens properly, rather than being hinge-like, involves a descent and forward action of the mandible or lower jaw (figures 6a, 6b and 6c). This helps to create the famous but not always understood "open throat" feeling. It also allows the tongue to be calm at the floor of the mouth, its tip present but not pressing against the back of the lower teeth. This is action, not relaxation. I draw it here: above, the skull; below, the jawbone/mandible at the Temporal-Mandibular Joint. To see it in proper anatomical context, look at Plate 11 in Netter's Atlas of Human Anatomy.

How, I hope you ask, can I be sure that I am doing this? First, find your state of balance and poise as explained earlier. Now open your mouth well and neutrally, as though about to yawn, and place your tongue over the lower lip and out as if it were going to proceed over your chin to your toes. Though exaggerated, your mouth is properly open. Please do not think of the flesh on

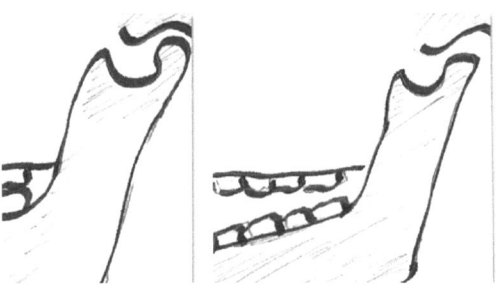 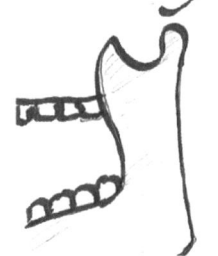

Fig. 6a — Jaw closed
Fig. 6b — Jaw slightly open
Fig. 6c — Jaw well-opened

the front of your face as your mouth. Your mouth is where your teeth, hard and soft palates and tongue exist. This placement of the tongue, at least atop the lower teeth or over the lower lip, is an important tonic for a proper mouth opening. To feel the movement, place each index finger just in front of the middle of each ear. If you then open your mouth as though yawning, you will feel the mandible descend, slide forward and as you extend the tongue outward in a downward arc, you will feel even more the forward slide of the jaw. Do this frequently, observing your body's responses, one place at a time, and you will build very helpful habits.

As you imagine a yawn, you will find yourself frequently yawning. Good! Study what you feel, piece by piece, place by place, until you clearly see what's moving and how. "Relax the jaw" or "drop the jaw" are counter-productive commands. They remove the poise from your vocal body and require an outward and downward expansion of the abdominal muscles in order to sustain tone: an action that leads to tightening of the thoracic diaphragm along with muscles of the neck and larynx.

Two related exercises and their generated movements which help you to feel the proper functioning of the jaw in a balanced vocal body are: 1) With your mouth open just short of a yawn, place your tongue just over your lower lip and sing scales, arpeggios or phrases (phrases without consonants for obvious reasons). Imagine that your tongue continues out and over your chin to the floor and that sound is not possible until contact, like electrical contact, of the tongue to the floor is made and maintained. 2) With your mouth equally open, instead of downward, imagine that your tongue extends out and upward until its tip contacts the tip of your nose; once again, sound being impossible until the contact is made and maintained. While working well with all vowels, this upward image is especially helpful in feeling the Italian I (ee) vowel. What does it all feel like?

An effective mind-game derived from these two images is to imagine that your tongue is forked vertically. **Mentally** extend it out of your mouth like a snake with one half or tine of its fork reaching up in an arc to touch your nose and the other reaching down likewise to touch your chin. See it in Figure 7. Imagine that and sing scales or exercises without consonants in order to feel a proper mouth opening. You can make a cartoon of yourself at any time for remarkably helpful feelings.

At separate times, study what the palatal arch (side-to-side between your ears, above the uvula) feels like (note how high it feels), what your lower jaw feels like (note the direction of intense energy in it), the front of your skull above the eyebrow, the back of your skull, the sides of your skull, the hard palate and mask of your face, your eyes, the area behind the center of each ear, your chest, your scapulas (shoulder blades), your ribcage, your lower abdomen. How do all these elements move and connect with one another and as a whole? Check them all out ***one at a time***.

Pick an area and you will notice a response there when you yawn. For instance, in the expanse of a yawn, imagine your tongue out over the upper lip; then over the lower lip. No change in the open jaw structure when the tongue thoughts are applied means that you are getting it. Become familiar with these elements of the singing body by repeated observation. Repetition creates understanding, habits of coordination, muscle memories and confidence.

Soon, when you open your mouth to sing you will feel yourself take on the sensation of yawning - everywhere. For a while, when you yawn, rather than just return to a closed mouth, release sound as though sighing and note your feelings. Play with that, always giving out in release, never trying to physically control.

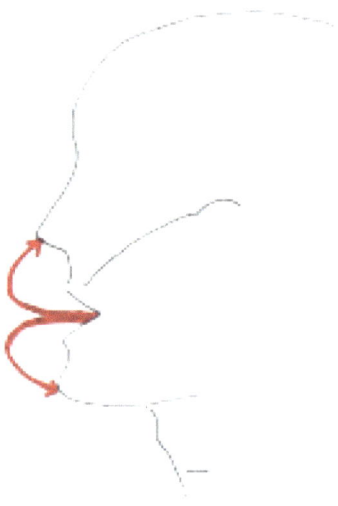

Fig. 7

KEEP ON HUMMIN'

THIS IS A PHOTO I took on Great Exuma in the Bahamas in the spring of 1988. Here solely as a segue, I call it "Hummin.'" It is difficult to overestimate humming's importance in understanding the resonance and structure of singing.

There are three types of humming in terms of vocalization, the first two being common: 1) the lips approximated for the sound of "m" as in hu<u>m</u> and 2) the tip of the tongue gently resting on the ridge of the hard palate immediately behind the upper front teeth, forming the sound "n" as in ma<u>n</u>.

The third, the open-mouthed hum, can be experienced by sustaining the <u>ng</u> at the end of the word "hung." When saying "hung" in a vocalizing context, do not bite down on the ng, but rather open to it as though you were about to a yawn. When you sing any pitch or phrase on "<u>ng</u>," you will eventually notice

CB=cheek bone
HP=hard palate
SP=soft palate
HB=hyoid bone
VC=vocal cords
CV7=7th cervical vertebra
CS=crown of sternum
T=tongue

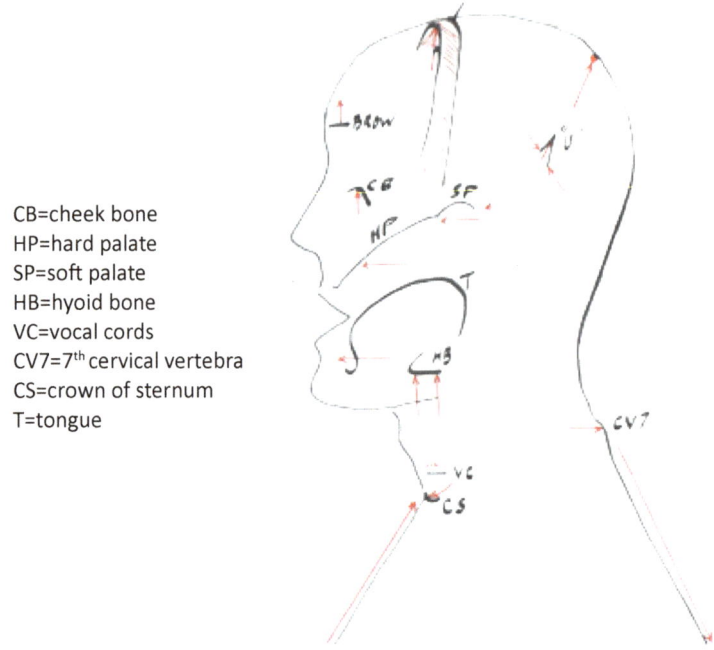

Fig. 8 Structural energies when yawning and the perceived pharyngeal adjustment with the thought of "U" (oo as in loot)

a strong upward energy with vibration/resonance at the arch where the hard palate meets the soft, at the bridge of the nose and a variety of locations throughout the skull. Enjoy them. Get to know them as friends and teachers.

Among those structural sensations is the perception of a band of strongly expansive energy and a wall of resistant membrane within it that you can perceive in the center of your head, spanning from side to side and reaching from the palatal arch to the top of the inside of your skull (Figure 8). See/feel just in front of and above your ears and including your temples to the top of your head. There is plenty of space between it and the inside of the front of your skull, a space I imagine to be the bell of you, the horn.

When you yawn, among the stronger feelings will be the rise of the palatal arch, seemingly between the jaw "hinges." Between that arch and the top of the back of the tongue there forms, in what seems like the middle of your head, an inner mouth - "middle mouth," if you will. That is the opening through which your sound is released, reflected, the end of your horn. Everything in front of it, cavities, bone, general anatomy of mouth and face, is the bell of the horn where resonance is refined, vowels and consonants articulated and imagined colors applied. Between the palatal arch and the back of your skull there is the sense of a cavernous ballooning space for resonance as well.

Imagine a wall, perceived as a membrane within the arc to the top of the skull, pictured in Figure 8. Mentally lean into it and notice all the energies and their directions indicated with arrows. These are *structural* energies/sensations, *not* the same as *resonant* energies. See them *one at a time* when you yawn naturally, or when you imagine and approach a yawn intentionally. The upward energy of the palatal arch and the perceived wall in the center of your head are sensations upon which all others depend, like the center pole of the circus tent.

There is an anchor energy at the crown of the sternum which seems to urge forward and down, another anchor urging backward at Cervical Vertebra (CV) 7, a strong forward energy in the chin between the lower teeth and the chin bone and at the jaw "hinge," upward energies at the cheek bones, the bridge of the nose, the tongue (hyoid) bone, the mastoid process, the upper molars and at the palatal arch.

Do not take this illustration or even my description for granted. Study the yawn in full expansion. When you do, notice what you feel immediately. Yawn again and feel again, one place and direction at a time. Do this until the senses of inflation and energies of expansion, as a complete and balanced structure, become the inevitable response to the intention to sing. Incorporate the feeling of your entire torso into your study of the yawn and note what you feel right down to your pelvic diaphragm, the floor of the torso.

To me it feels as though from the hips through my feet, I am planted and connected to the center of the earth, while simultaneously, beginning with the pelvic diaphragm, the upper half of me, the "inflated" half, wants to lift upward off the hips (Figure 9 ahead).

During my graduate study at Juilliard, a wonderful bass-baritone, Chester Watson, who was the bass soloist at St. James Episcopal where I was the tenor, once said to me that singing feels just like yawning. It was some years later when I began to understand the pithy importance of his sage advice. *The open-mouthed hum, derived from the yawn and the word, huNG will show you the structural sensations in the mouth and pharynx that foster ease in singing and clarity of resonance.*

A wind instrument, except for the French horn and flute/piccolo/recorder, sports a mouthpiece with one or two reeds, an inception point for the creation of sound. It's not much of a stretch to see ourselves as a double reed instrument like the bassoon, oboe, English horn and others whose reeds are set into vibration by the application of the lips, carefully guided by the technically trained mouth and musical mind.

We must prepare the reed, our vocal cords, and apply our musical imaginations to begin and continue the playing. Figure 8 shows the imagined high point inside the back top of your skull. I drew it with a red arrow and dot. It can also be felt as the upper end of the arc described in Figure 3. It is structural: the center pole of the circus tent, as I said. The height you feel inside to that point gives tensile stretch to the vocal cords and cannot be overrated. See it. Feel it as the upper back-most point of the yawn. *Mentally* maintain it, *but do not attempt to make it happen.*

A word of caution here might avoid a common tension-producing misunderstanding. The body's natural response to the thought of the arc from head to coccyx is a lengthening of the spine and a very gentle tilt, up and ever so slightly back, of the head. *It happens.* You don't intentionally move your head back. It feels as though you "join" the arc. The result brings the skull to balance on the spine, allowing muscles of the neck freedom from having to hold up the head. It also lifts the ribcage as in Figure 2. You must maintain the inflated feeling of the head and torso as a shape, the balloon, hips-to-head; that is your carriage wanting to float above the pelvis while your legs, hips-to-soles, are planted where you stand. Awareness of the pelvic diaphragm is enough. Conscious manipulation of it is overkill and will create destructive tension.

Another thought process that engenders the sense of the whole instrument is, within the context of the carriage that you feel with the imagined arc, to think of the lowest pitch that you can and notice the body's response. With that added to the carriage, think of the highest pitch that you can imagine. Notice that response, particularly in the head. Maintain the high-low feelings and sing straight through the apex of the triangle resulting from the thought of "U" - scales, melodies, single tones, whatever. I have indicated in Figure 8 the approximate location of the sensation of the coming together of the top of a triangle with the thought of the vowel "U" as in "loot." Just think "U" in a yawn's expansiveness. When you play the clarinet, you are aware of its entirety from top to bottom. Why not the body when singing?

Notice that a smooth, side-to-side movement of the head at any time with arc #5 (page 26) open can help to release tension in the back of the neck and the upper back.

> Everything that we observe regarding the movement of parts in the pharynx and front of the mouth and about sensations of resonance and tone columns is predicated upon a flexible expansive structure within your head, which feels like the expansion inside a well-inflated balloon, or when yawning.

THE BREATH WHEN SINGING

Dr. P. Mario Marafioti, M.D., was Enrico Caruso's vocal physician and the author of a volume entitled Caruso's Method of Voice Production.[7] That book was wholly endorsed by Enrico Caruso, who remains unsurpassed in the history of operatic tenors for technical mastery, power, emotional colors, artistry and consistency. Dr. Marafioti describes seven principles which guided Caruso's understanding of the voice and singing. The third of these is that breath, while indispensable, is not the prime cause of good tone. Contrary to much teaching, it is well-imagined tone that draws the breath into play and through repetition builds stamina and power into the breathing apparatus.

Management of the breath is part of but not the crux of easy singing. Management of the pitch mechanism, the vocal cords, is the centerpiece of all vocal emission. Breathing for singing is a complex coordination, but disarmingly simple when learned. Mentally maintaining vocal cord adduction is 99% of your goal, but *physically attempting to control any one aspect of breathing while singing can lead to seriously destructive imbalance and tension.* I had learned and understood this before I read Dr. Marafioti, so you can imagine the feeling of validation that I enjoyed having found it there.

Think about the balloon: As children and young-at-heart adults, most of us have blown up balloons and pressed the lips closed with both hands, holding the air within. If we release one of our hands on the lips, air escapes, causing a loose vibration of the lips. If we press tightly and stretch the lips to obtain a small opening, we get a vibrational frequency related to the air pressure below and the tension, length, thickness and opening of the lips, which becomes a note, whine or sound in the environment. Adjust the stretch, size and consequent opening of the lips and we can get a few pitches. At no time can we squeeze the balloon or we will distort nature's balance between pressure, the air in the balloon, and resistance: the adjusted opening of the lips. Extraneous pressure leads directly to unintended pitch, distorted timbre and no control.

Think about the garden hose: Take a simple garden hose. Attach the hose to a faucet and turn the water on. Now hold the hose up without a nozzle. The column of water will be as wide as the hose's internal diameter, will go so high and at a particular speed or intensity. Attach the nozzle and you have reduced the opening available for the water to escape the hose. The column of water will now be reduced in diameter and increased in distance and speed or intensity. The more you reduce the size of the opening, the higher, faster and thinner the column. All the while, it is not necessary to adjust the faucet.

Likewise, the energy of compressed air in the lungs against the vocal cords must remain constant. Once you have allowed air to return to your lungs (inhaled or replenished) and engaged your intention to sing, you have effectively turned on the faucet. Now you are the vehicle for the sound's emission. You are not the source. Your imagination is the source.

> "SINGING DEVELOPS THE BREATH; NOT THE BREATH, SINGING."[4]

In a balanced, coordinated vocal body, air supply is kept constant against the pitch mechanism - the vocal cords - by a flexible diaphragm, released into a domed shape in automatic response to the thought of phonation and by the adduction or approximation of the vocal cords maintained. Conscious upward, downward or outward pressure of the diaphragm is the same as opening the faucet further in order to affect a more intense stream of water or, looking back at the first example, squeezing the balloon; unnecessary, it distorts nature's way. A common technique of holding a book between your diaphragm and a wall as you sing is begging for distortion and tension as well. Actually, conscious physical attempts to release the diaphragm also can upset nature's flow. Let it be.

Without a constant, indispensable minimum breath pressure, it is likely that you will present either too little or too much pressure for a given pitch. The resulting maladjustment of the vocal cords will cause tension around the neck and larynx and subsequently the entire body; which tension, like a narcotic, must be applied in greater amounts to maintain the desired result until the body breaks down under the strain. One fine day, given mindful work with the proper exercises, you will be able to sing chromatically from your lowest note to your highest with a single breath pressure.

There is a fascinating correlation between the rise of the soft palate, the thoracic diaphragm, and a complex of muscles and tendons forming what is known as the pelvic diaphragm, the strong and flexible floor of your abdomen. Have a look at figure 9.

> A happy result of understanding a single breath pressure is the realization that there is only one register. There is no break in your scale, no "passaggio". Every pitch is a passaggio, an everywhere adjustment of the vocal cords and the body, a passage to the next pitch higher or lower.

When you yawn, among many other feelings, there is the sensation of a lift into what feels like a cavernous space between the ears, behind and above the palatal arch. If you maintain that feeling after the yawn has passed and pay attention to the pelvic and the thoracic diaphragms, you will notice that each seems to be domed upward. **Mentally** connect the soft palate, the flexible top of the perceived cavernous space, to the pelvic diaphragm and you will have connected two of the most important dots on the grid. The thoracic diaphragm will function as it always does in a healthy body: automatically, without conscious effort. You don't consciously pull the pelvic diaphragm into a dome either. The connection is mental, a product of awareness when seeing the entire instrument.

This is where a large number of singing instructors miss so important a point: the connection to the lower abdomen. Before I met Jim Carson, I studied with one, a popular teacher in New York City who taught that an intentional drawing in of the lower abdominal muscles, like the squeezing of a toothpaste tube, would help propel the breath upward to the vocal cords in "support" of the diaphragm and so, tone. When this teacher sang to demonstrate a note or phrase, the back of the tongue flapped rapidly like a flag in a 50-mph gale. That was enormous tension from a misapplied concept. Like all teachers, the intention was well-meant, but like so many, the information was ill-conceived or misunderstood.

Through mindful application of the exercises presented at the end of this book, particularly numbers 1 and 2, you can develop a clear image of the thought-generated singing position in the mouth/pharynx, a flexible, ever-adjusting structure governing the body's brace, the vocal cords' accurate adjustment and the optimal receptor/reflector for the tonal column in the pharynx: pitch thought 1, cord adjustment 1, pharyngeal adjustment 1, body brace 1; pitch thought 2, cord adjustment 2, pharyngeal adjustment 2, body brace 2, and so on throughout your range.

You think the pitch/vowel, observe the physical responses everywhere from above and behind with your mind's eye and allow the sound to be released through the thought-adjusted instrument. In time your memory of the various pitch adjustments yields a tactile sense of the pitches bordering on "perfect." You learn the feel of a note. Be mindful that, as in the garden hose metaphor, the breath pressure must remain a constant indispensable minimum throughout your range.

While singing and taking "catch" breaths or during long periods of rest, breathe through your mouth and/or nose, and by that I mean the opening at the front of your skull as though the nostrils and cartilage that is your visible nose did not exist. Perhaps a better word for breathing while singing is "replenishing." Each opening of the cords releases a tiny vortex of air, frequent according to the pitch and duration; air which must be replenished in obedience to nature (abhorring a vacuum).

As an exercise, expel as much of your lungs' air as possible through pursed lips and then just open your mouth and be aware of your nose as the larger opening without nostrils (see Fig. 13). The lungs replenish the spent air without intentional inhaling. Make that a habit and vary the rhythm of replenishing and expelling in order to enjoy tension-free breathing while singing.

So that there is no confusion, please understand that an "indispensable minimum" of breath pressure is that which comes naturally for the lowest note in your range. What becomes more intense as pitches rise up the scale of frequencies is the resonance excited by the ever increasing number of vibrations naturally occurring from a decreasing opening in the vocal folds, not an increase in air flow or pressure.

If you are not pushing, pulling, lifting or depressing anything, what, you may ask, does breath "pressure" feel like? Imagine that you are going to swim a lap under water. Open your mouth just short of a yawn and draw air in noiselessly through your nose and mouth. Feel like a balloon? Good. Since you are theoretically swimming underwater, you are active but not releasing air, not exhaling. That's one way the singing body feels.

Another is to bend forward at the waist to about 30 degrees, back straight, keeping your chin parallel to the floor as though placed on a table before you. Now inhale with a tone in mind and sing whole phrases or exercises in this position, noticing how you feel head to hip. What moves and how? What does that feel like? Stand up very slowly while maintaining the feelings. What's that like?

Yet another is to imagine a line descending from your ear out across your shoulder. Turn your head without turning your shoulders, keeping it straight up, and look back behind the line from your ear, which seems to divide the shoulder into anterior and posterior halves. Singing exercises or whole phrases of music in this position is a powerful tonic to help you feel all aspects of the singing body. I will demonstrate this for your clarity on the DVD.

In figure 9, see the inter-relationship of the pelvic diaphragm, the thoracic diaphragm and the hard and soft palates, which work in tandem with one another. All jump to attention and poise in the well-trained vocal body when the thought of the approximated triangle sides at the top of what I call the long arc is willed in. Note the upward and downward energies at the hips and the top and bottom of the long arc, respectively. These aspects of the instrumental body can be observed one-at-a-time. Begin with the long arc, then open open the mouth as though about to yawn and with your awareness behind your head, see the triangle at the top of the arc close and remain so. When you do, observe the whole body, head to hips.

An important way to understand the nature of the pelvic diaphragm is to imagine a ball or wheel spinning backward. The thought of it spinning helps to avoid holding anything or forcing any action in the lower abdomen, to maintain an even breath pressure and to give you a sense of being grounded. Figure 10 shows a turbine-like energy, spinning as indicated, encountering no resistance, increasing in speed with the frequency of the pitch, giving lift to the pelvic diaphragm and a weightless but firm foundation to the singing body. Of equal importance is the anchoring of downward energy of the arc into the tailbone.

> Important Habit: Mentally sing while you replenish your breath. That way you remain in the singing position and allow air to return to the lungs rather than physically trying to draw it in.

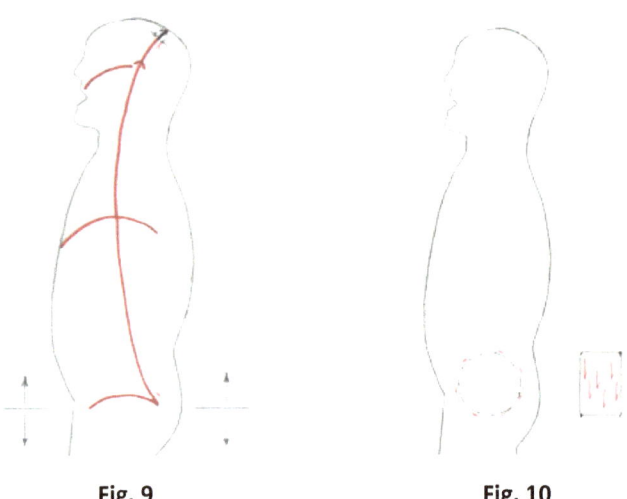

Fig. 9　　　　　　　　Fig. 10

PHONATION

PHONATION IS A PSYCHO-NEURAL EXPERIENCE, a product of your will. How do you will in the sound you want to make? Voice teachers commonly advise that a singer must hear each note before singing it. Good advice, but what does that mean? Must I hear every note? All the time? How does that guarantee my sound? How much can I think about at one time? One thing at a time is all you need consider as you build the habits that serve you when performing. A little chip here, a little there, and before long the statue emerges from the block. An impersonator listens to and mimics the sounds of his subject, practicing colors, gestures and carriage in minute detail. Why not listen in your imagination to the voice you want to hear and release it as though in mimicry? Here is a brick-by-brick strategy for developing the ability to see and feel the voice as response to thought.

When you imagine a pitch, vowel, color, or dynamic, your vocal body responds instantaneously to create it in your physical reality. If you are a natural singer, you will produce exactly what you imagined. Anything less than what you intended means that you have to further train the body's response mechanism.

In performance, provided that your vocal body has been trained well, thinking a measure or phrase ahead while singing will be all that's necessary. In the studio, building the vocal body and your awareness, you must slowly and deliberately drill the thought-response process, note by note. Among the exercises in Appendix E you will find The Great Scale. For any style of singing it should be your "teacher away from the lesson."

The thought of any pitch will result in an adjustment of the pharynx to an exact size and place to receive or accommodate the tone column for that pitch (more about tone columns soon). Likewise, the thought of a vowel will engender an exact shape in the mouth/pharynx to express the vowel intended.

The singer's objective is to become aware of the changes for each vowel and each pitch by slowing the thought-to-feeling process. Soon you will clearly see the changed size/shape/position of each note in your range and each vowel. Provided that all structural - skull, pharynx, mouth - criteria are met, hearing a note becomes an exercise in feeling.

During a yawn's expansiveness, you can point and move an index finger straight upward close to and beside either ear and be able to feel a strong stretch upward in the middle of your head and a lift of the mask - cheekbones, nose, forehead. That action enables you to sing your entire range. When you are tired or distracted, the height of the vertical stretch inside is frequently the first structural element to be compromised, making the high and upper-middle notes of your range difficult, if not impossible, to sing without 'pushing.' See this "tool" in Appendix B.

The structural integrity of you, the instrument, must never be compromised. You would not adjust the shape of your clarinet as you played it. Parts within it are constantly moving, but it's always the clarinet. Likewise, your poise, your sense of hollowness head to hip, your feeling of the flexible structure within your head, must remain as you sing while all else is in flow, no two notes with exactly the same feeling anywhere. This is done with *thought,* with *imagination,* not by holding anything.

TONE COLUMNS

EACH PITCH IN YOUR RANGE is a specific frequency, which translates to a number of openings and closings of the vocal cords per second. Each opening releases a vortex of air like an invisible smoke ring. On A-440, the A above middle C, for instance, the vocal cords open and close 440 times per second. That action creates a sound wave/column, the top of which is felt in the pharynx, not unlike a splash-point were you to hold an object above the garden hose mentioned earlier.

You cannot feel the columns, but you can feel their tops. As the pitch/frequency rises, the columns become narrower and the sensations of their tops smaller and more intense. You cannot successfully "place" the feelings but with repetition you can remember them, seeing them with your mind's eye while physically allowing their procession within the flexible structure of the mouth/pharynx. Some like to imagine the vowels on the tops of the columns as though each were a platform, diminishing in size while increasing in intensity.

Shall I compare thee to a flashlight? Your energy/Qi/life-force is the battery or power source. Pushing the switch is tantamount to exciting the vocal cords in response to a pitch thought; the top of the tonal column is the lit bulb wherever you feel it; everything above, behind and in front of the top of the column is the cone of the flashlight, amplifying the light. The sound that others hear is the light on the wall. The "bulb," your articulation, coloring of vowels and interior sensations ALONE are your responsibility.

The sound that you emit is now subject to the environment. The same note sung in an identical manner would be very differently perceived in a closet, Carnegie Hall or a gymnasium. You can only stand and deliver as the instrument in the moment.

Not understanding the previous paragraph can be a major miscalculation for most singers. Unconsciously or consciously adjusting to a lack of resonant return in a "dry" performance space, the singer might beef up the sound. The more you give heft to the sound, the more you inhibit your own resonance and the less can come back to your ears: the proverbial vicious circle.

The remedy is always to remain aware of yourself, the instrument. Sing the sound that you imagine in the moment and let the space be the space. In performance you are always creating. *Leave the listening to the audience.* Observe your feelings in flow as they respond to your imagination's concept of the music.

Following in Figure 11 is a drawing of the relative sensations of the tone column tops. In Figure 12 you see the notes where the sensations begin and continue. It is almost 100% accurate, though some feel the ascent behind the vertical beginning on D, 4th line, rather than Eb, 4th space. Observe, discover and remember.

Singing: Nature's Gift To You | 59

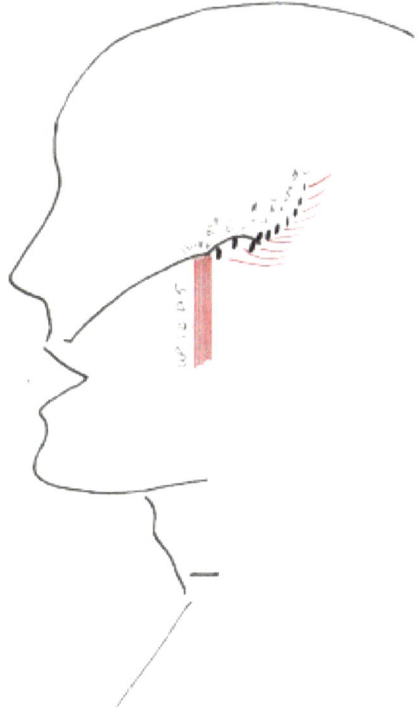

Fig. 11 Column Tops

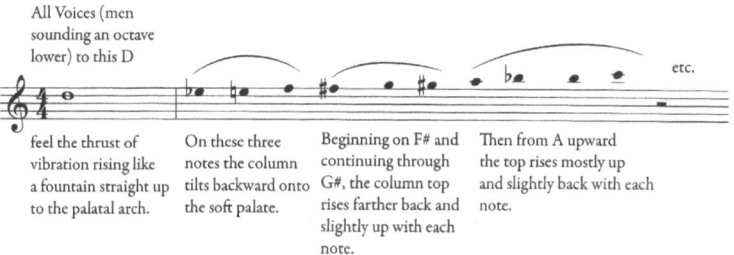

Fig. 12 Column Tops

AWARENESS EXERCISES

First - and at once foremost, back-most and up-most - imagine a narrow triangle at the top of the arc illustrated in Figure 3, p. 28. Not more than an inch or so long, imagine that the sides of the triangle come together, adduct. Maintain the adduction. Focus on that alone within your hollowness. See it as pictured in Figure 5, p. 32. Play with it by opening and closing the triangle with your imagination. Do not attempt anything physical, but take note of anything physical resulting from this moving image.

While everything in the structure of the instrument always must be free to move, one constant, fixed star when singing or preparing to sing should be the apex of the slender triangle or cone, felt above and behind the path of tonal platforms or column tops; the sensation of an upward energy, high in the head *perceived* as wanting to press through the skull at the posterior fontanelle. It will be seen and then felt more clearly over time with repetition of the thought of "U" (Oo as in "root") in a yawn's expansiveness. I refer you again to Figure 8 on p. 40.

Second, induce a yawn and feel the stretch of the mouth/pharynx cavity. What do you feel in the center of your head, extending upward from the juncture of the hard and soft palates between each jaw hinge, that seems to want to push through the top of the skull in an arc from ear to ear? What does it feel like from the center of the ear-to-ear arc down to the ridge of the hard palate just above and behind the upper front teeth? What do you feel in the jawbone just under the front teeth? What do you feel at the nose (not the fleshy part but the thin bone that forms the 'bridge' of the nose and the opening seen ahead in Figure 13)? How about at the hard palate and the front of your skull right up to the hairline? What do you feel in the area of the jaw "hinge," the Temporal Mandibular Joint (TMJ)? What about the upper jaw and teeth, left and right? Where do you feel expansive space?

Keep these feelings alive in your mind's eye, not by holding anything, but rather by imagining that the yawn/stretch energy is continuing in all directions. Do not try to notice them all at once, but repeat the yawn sensation and look at them one at a time. Be patient. Like the stars at night, the longer you look the more you will see.

Third, feeling the yawn-like structure, think of and sing a median pitch in your range: the A below or middle C for men; the C an octave higher for women. Where do you feel vibrations? Where do you feel resonance? Intersect those vibrations by an imagined vertical line from the top center of your head, passing immediately in front of the ear and proceeding to your pelvis.

From your lowest note to the D above middle C, the thrust of the tonal columns seems to be centered at the palatal arch immediately at or in front of the imagined vertical line. That is not to say that you don't feel vibrational excitement at the roof of the mouth, the bridge of the nose, the sinuses and elsewhere. It's just that a primary resonance/vibration is evident in the center of the raised palatal arch. Beginning on E-flat, ½ step higher, top space on the treble clef, the sensation of pitch vibration, resonance or energy — the "splash point" that is the top of the tonal column - moves slightly back of the vertical and up under the soft palate behind the palatal arch, continuing that path through F, top line of the treble clef, which sounds an octave lower in men.

On F# the sensation of the top of the tone column seems to break through the soft palate, reaching up into the head. On G the sensation continues its journey into the head in a mostly back and slightly upward path.

The movement of the top-of-the-column sensation from pitch to pitch changes to a mostly up and slightly back direction from A-flat to A and on up as illustrated in Figure 11. It is very important to maintain the sense of open space between your awareness and the tops of the columns. This allows their unimpeded rise. Study figures 11 and 12 to see again what I just described.

Scale work, particularly the Great Scale, helps you see and feel the path of the column tops. You mindfully **allow** their passage into the head. You cannot move them physically or place them with any intentional muscular action without risking serious tension. In time you will know exactly how a given note feels at the very thought of it. The thought of a scale without audible sound yields the feelings of singing as well.

I have developed a kind of tactile perfect pitch in that the thought of a note engenders all the pertinent feelings throughout the body, head and mouth for any vowel, and I sing through that adjustment. It seems uncannily accurate, but it isn't uncanny. It's just unusual because few will take the time to develop this level of awareness. All that I can say is that it is well worth the effort.

Fourth, with the jaw "properly open" as though yawning, think of the vowel a (ah, as in "far"). Vowels are not shaped by the lips, which must remain neutral, as when yawning. When you think of a vowel, with your mouth in a neutral, well-opened, quasi-yawn position you will feel a physical response in two easily-sensed places: the area of the upper back of your mouth, your pharynx, just behind and above the palatal arch, and in the groove that runs up from the ridge of the hard palate behind the upper teeth to the palatal arch, seemingly behind the nose.

With your lips neutral as in the sensation of a yawn, think of e (eh, as in "let") without a pitch in mind. Note the action in the pharynx and what happens with the tongue, hard and soft palates. Then i (ee as in "need"), o (oh as in "boat"), u (oo as in "loot"), ü as in the German "müde," ö as in the German "Flöte," and so on for any vowel sound in any language. The thought of a vowel creates movement-to-form, obedient to nature's needs.

That is mechanical function of the vocal body in response to thought. There is a sense of the same action for the formation of any vowel high in the pharynx. With the vowel u (oo, as in "loot"), for example, you feel a coming together high in the pharynx and a similar action, the sensation of the size of a straw, at the front of the hard palate.

In figure 13 you see the area of most vivid vibration/resonance of the mask. It yields the "chiaro" of your tone. These feelings are part of the refinement of your sound, the reflective cone in the flashlight metaphor, *not* the source; nor is any single area more important than any other. These sensations are the result of accurately seen and felt tops of tone columns. Trying to "place" your voice in the mask or anywhere else is tantamount to putting the cart before the horse.

Fig. 13 The nose as far as singers should be concerned. When excited by vibrations of resonance, it yields the "chiaro" of your timbre, the higher overtones or partials.

When I speak of breathing through the nose, it is the opening in Figure 13 that is the portal. In your imagination nothing should exist in front of it. Your replenishment of air should seem to pass through the upper arch of that opening, the bridge of the nose. Even when breathing through the mouth, a sense of lift from the top of this nose opening to the hairline can be felt. Take careful note of the feelings at the opening when you yawn. Once again, the yawn is critical in understanding structural integrity in the vocal body.

In the maximum yawn stretch, think of a pitch in the middle of your range and notice the physical reaction in your mouth, pharynx, and torso. Then hear-in-order-to-feel a pitch a fourth higher in the scale, then an octave higher than that. Study the feelings and the changes. Now think of the lowest note in your range and feel particularly the response in your pelvic diaphragm. Maintaining that feeling, mentally hear the highest pitch that you can and become aware of the point high in your head where it seems to want to pierce through the top of your skull.

A simultaneous sense of the lowest and highest pitches

in your range gives you the feeling, top to bottom of you, the instrument. Develop and keep that feeling for stability and balance, not only of the vocal body in general, but of the vocal cords themselves. With that particular awareness, the cords are stretched to a thinness and proper tension with the trachea lifted back and up allowing the "chiaro" (light) of your sound, and the thyroid cartilage is gently tilted forward and down, permitting the "scuro" (darkness or shadow) of your sound.

As the pitch rises, the tops of the tonal columns seem to "grip" or lean on the columns firmly like a cap. It feels like a tiny version of the figure, ^, with this v sitting atop *that*: much like this appearance: ⋈. The first image represents the risen energy of the tonal column; the second, sitting atop the first, the mental resistance of equal energy. This is "l'appoggia," a noun derived from the Italian verb, appoggiare, meaning to lean or rest upon (go figure…). All is seen from behind with what? THE MIND'S EYE. Allow and observe.

There are opposing energies everywhere in your body when you sing. The tops of the columns are the only points of mental resistance that will not produce harmful tension.

It is of paramount importance that your mental presence behind the domed palate and column tops, within a tension-free but maximally expanded structure, must never be distracted. Read the last sentence again several times. It is the constant *mental presence, not physical pressing* of the vowel thought, against the upper back of the palatal arch or top of the tonal column, depending on pitch, that maintains a constant breath pressure against the vocal cords from the lungs beneath.

The presence at the top of the tone column resists the upward energy of the tone column rising from the vocal cords in direct proportion. As this column top or palatal energy accepts the thrust of airwaves generated by the various opening and closing frequencies of the vocal cords, you can see how Italians and others who practiced this technique would have described it as "leaning on the breath."

> A revealing exercise: With everything of your vocal body structure in place (inflatedness, arcs, highest and lowest note sensations, adduction image), focus on what's in front of you with the eyes on the front of your face. Now switch to your mind's eye and focus on the "U" vowel apex described in Figure 8 on page 40. What happens? Alternate your awareness between them until the difference is stark. It's all right to exclaim: "Aha!"

Another observation as the pitch rises above the staff is that the columns become narrower and their tops more intense, like a splash-point above a garden hose flow. The sensation may seem to be that you are adding breath pressure, but in fact you are only equally resisting the rising energy of the column or beam, leaning on it with mental presence.

Physically, when you lean toward the palatal arch or column top, the soft palate is not so subtly being lifted automatically. Become aware of the center of your pelvis when you do this and you will notice its movement in tandem with the soft palate. Every element of our physical bodies acts in flow and interdependence with every other in constant response to our thoughts. We are a musical instrument.

Over time, the tops of the tonal columns will be felt as an unmistakable small firm platform on which a vowel can be placed. Looking back at Figures 11 and 12, I repeat that for most voices the tone columns leading to and including D, 4th line of the treble clef, feel thrust up to the palatal arch from the vocal cords below. The journey into the head begins on the Eb, 4th space of the treble clef. These feelings exist within a constantly adjusting "instrument." To see more clearly what's happening here, imagine a median line from your neck out over and across your shoulder. Keeping your shoulders aligned with hips and squared forward, look over one shoulder to a point behind that median line. Open your mouth well with the thought of A (ah) and observe the shape of your mouth from ears to front teeth. Notice also the sense of space between and behind your ears. Think the vowels Ee, Eh, Ah, Oh, Oo (Italian = i-e-a-o-u), first mentally and then vocally, spoken and sung. Notice the movements and energies with each vowel change.

Sing the vowels in this position from G, second line of the treble clef (noticing the movements and energies with each vowel) to G above the staff, one note at a time. Basses and baritones should take the scale at least to Eb. The more you do this, the more clearly you will see and feel the actions. Do this to either side (alternating sides is a good idea) for as long as it takes to see/feel clearly. The side-to-side movement of your head should be easy and smooth to avoid tension.

This work is for the purpose of developing proper function. If you were a trumpet, your awareness would be your person behind and at the mouthpiece, holding the trumpet, directing the sound with your imagination. The tops of the columns are the adjusting sizes and intensities that would be your lips on the mouthpiece.

All the moving pieces on the structure that is a trumpet would be the moving pieces that you have discovered in/on you, head to hip. The horn would end where your palatal arch above and tongue below define an opening like an inner mouth, situated between your ears. I repeat that all in front of that "middle mouth" is similar to the bell of the horn: the refiner of resonance.

Once you understand the previous paragraph, the sounds that you release will seem to be detached, like a holographic image dancing free of tether between your hairline and your tongue bone (hyoid). The rays extending forward from the palatal arch and the tops of the columns are resonance, not source. They are the three-dimensional image of the hologram, the reflective cone of the flashlight.

The tops of the columns can be metaphorically the gems through which the holographic images are focused, or the constantly shifting bulb of a flashlight. Do I repeat myself? Given the confusion surrounding so important a truth, it deserves repeating many times, many ways.

Do not sing into the so-called mask of your skull/face. Rather, with your awareness behind your head looking forward and through, sing into the entire front of your head through the raised palatal arch allowing and observing the tops of the tone columns rising like shifting pinpoint targets. Imagine directing an electrical current like a beam, not a flow of energy as in a wind tunnel or a water cannon burst.

Every image, every sensation is singularly important when focusing on it during development, but none is more important than any other when feeling the entire instrument in performance. That said, once all is balanced, strong and flexible, the focus on any one element will accurately engage all elements. On a given day you may need to pay attention to one aspect or another for whatever reason and for however long, but you can be assured that balance will out and the complete instrument will function in seamless coordination when tuning is done.

VOWEL MODIFICATION

It is impossible to overestimate the importance of modifying the vowel *thought* as pitches rise into your upper-middle and high range. The most complete study of this technique that I have found is that of E. Herbert-Caesari in his seminal book, The Voice of the Mind.[8]

We have already seen that the tonal columns narrow as the frequency of vibration rises. When you think of "ah," then "oo," you can feel the narrowing high in the pharynx and on the hard palate. So it follows that we can aid the narrowing of the columns by modifying our concept of the vowels. This begins for most singers on E flat, 4th space on the treble clef (tenors and baritones sounding an octave below sopranos and altos). Some feel this beginning on D. Each must find his or her own optimal adjustments. In the table we are referring to the treble clef.

The table shows the most effective vowel/thought modifications. What you can never forget is that only your thought of the vowel changes. You are doomed to tension if you physically shape the vowels. Of course there is physical change. That's the point, but it must be in response to thought, not your ego's sense of how a vowel should be shaped. Have you heard this enough yet?

Here's one thing that can separate will-be from wannabe: in the internal yawn-like expansiveness of the singing position — what you feel when saying or singing the ng in the word "hung" — you *allow* the pure vowel **formation** throughout your range with all the normal tongue and palate adjustments, maintaining the expansiveness of the inflated head-to-hip you, while thinking the variations when appropriate. It is the vowel thought that has the effect of reducing the size of the column top, not conscious shaping of the mouth/pharynx.

Why is this important? It is important because a sure way to create imbalance and negative tension is to intentionally "cover" the voice or vowel sound by physically changing the shape of your mouth to something narrower, more "rounded," especially near the so-called "breaks" in the voice around Eb or F#. The technique-become-art of mentally altering the vowel thought without reducing the sense of opening of the "middle mouth" achieved with the NG of the word, hung, effects the size of tone columns at their tops, giving them the narrowing points of acceptance in the pharynx commensurate with their natural decrease in diameter as the frequency of pitches increases.

Vowel Thought	Above D, 4th Line	Above Staff
AH becomes	Aw to Oh	"pUt" to Oo
Eh becomes	ö	Smaller ö
Ee becomes	ü	Smaller ü
Oh becomes	(remains) Oh	"pUt" to Oo
Oo becomes	U as in "put"	Smaller "pUt"

TUNING THE INSTRUMENT

I PREFER THE TERM *TUNING* to warming up. You warm up an engine. You tune a musical instrument. I know that it's just semantics, but I put great store in the different pictures our minds create when we say one thing or another.

Stand at ease and imagine that there is a thin strong band forming an arc from the upper back of your head to your tail bone (Fig. 3). Notice your spine, the way your head rests upon it, your ribcage. Imagine yourself as hollow from the top of your head to your hips; not a hollowness as in a void, but emptiness within an inflation so that there is a *sense* of equal presence/energy against your "shell" in an outward direction everywhere, like being an inflated balloon. Breathe slowly through your mouth and nose, seeing the air enter through your nasal opening, not your nostrils (see Fig. 11), to fill your ribcage as though it were a large bell.

Women will fill their lungs in one smooth movement. Men will notice a second element as the upper chest fills just under the neck after the lower "bell" has expanded. Watch the air enter as though drawn in by the descending diaphragm. As you exhale imagine your body continuing to expand. If you ever drew back the plunger of a syringe, the action is similar. Unlike a syringe, however, do not press upward at the thoracic diaphragm in order to expel the air. ***It is utilized automatically by each opening of the cords.*** As you do this, open your mouth as though to yawn, and imagine expansion of your head-to-hip balloon in all directions.

Open your mouth neutrally and well as you exhale and maintain the image and energy of the adducted vocal cords (Fig.5, p.31), noticing the paradox of the feeling of expansion even when exhaling. Thus, there is a pulse-like expansion of your entire head and torso upon inhaling and exhaling. **All the while it is most important to ask yourself: "What does this feel like?"** The picture is just that, but the feeling that it generates is what presses the emotional button and turns memory into knowledge. This is calming, centering, stress-relieving and the single best breathing habit you can learn for singing and for life, in my opinion.

With your awareness behind your hollow self, look forward at the palatal arch, the roof of the mouth and the opening of the nose. Maintaining that, think the vowel "a" as in bat. That will result in a gentle lift of the entire front of the face/skull, including the cheek bones.

Add to the senses of lifts of the arch and the mask the thought of U (oo as in "root") and notice the strong "coming together" in the upper back of the pharynx; again, this top of the triangle or cone wants to press up to the skull. These are constantly adjusting physical responses to thoughts and show you the structure within your head that is the physical vocal instrument. Do not try to effect these feelings with any deliberate muscular action.

One deliberate action that can help you understand the movement of parts and connections is: raise your index finger straight up beside your head just in front of an ear repeatedly while sustaining three thoughts simultaneously: the voiced nasal consonant <u>NG</u> as in the word huNG, then A as in "bat," then "U" ("oo"). Each time that you do this, notice the upward urgency to the skull and the entire mouth/pharynx area. Make a very close friend of that coordination (see it in Appendix B).

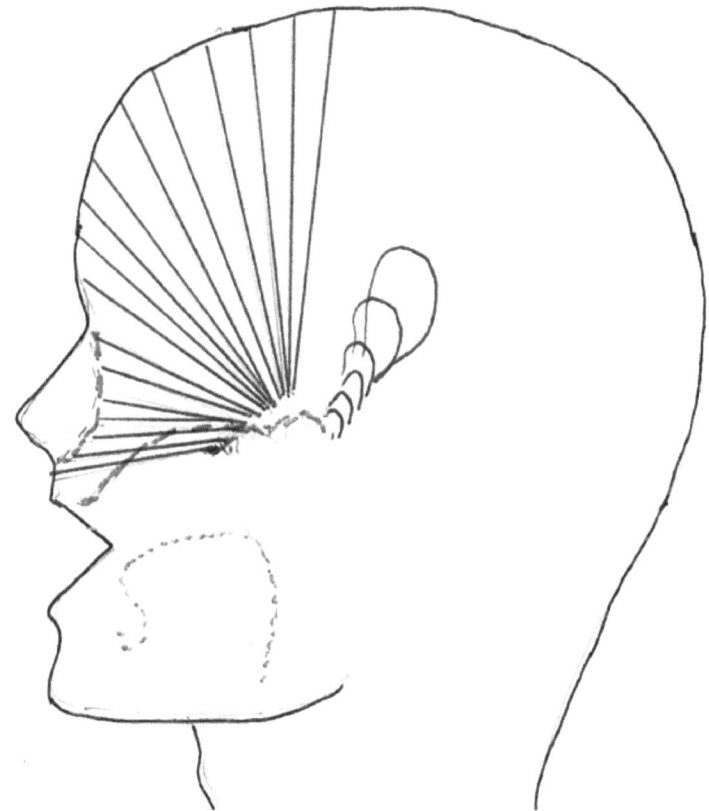

Fig. 14 Resonant sensations or energies, including the balloons of resonance that form atop the tonal columns as they rise above the staff — F# and up.

MOMENTUM

MOMENTUM IN SINGING IS A *continuous and forward-moving* energy, with your imagination as the power source. It's as though the intent to sing creates a living, moving beam or wave of sound which does not cease until after the last note of the piece. It has no altitude or depth, only speed and size, and is powered by your imagination. The higher the pitch, the faster the speed and smaller the diameter; the lower the pitch, the slower the speed and larger the diameter, but the momentum is always forward and the diameter of the beam perceived no greater than about 3/8". As the pitches rise in frequency and the column tops come into sensation, please remember that you cannot manipulate or try to draw the column tops back and up. Through repetition you will be able to re-member them as the thought of each pitch shows them to you clearly. I hyphenate the word "remember" because what you are doing when you re-member is re-creating a moment, giving it strength as you experience it again with your imagination, bringing it into your "now." Wrap your mind around that, please.

As you "ride" this sound-beam, you must think of (see) the coming note, measure or phrase but not what has passed, or any other distraction. Your consciousness must be focused singularly on what you are doing as "instrumentalist." This level of concentration requires long hours of contemplation and practice and is best experienced after structural form of the vocal body is more clearly understood. Focus on the target, one small goal at a time, undaunted by results which may fall short. If a note in the middle of an exercise falls out of the pattern of momentum, do not "pick it up" there. Return to the beginning of the exercise and see it through from mindful breath to the space beyond the cessation of sound. Momentum begins before the first note and continues beyond the last.

On the grander scale, your practicing, your development momentum day to day is just as important as what you feel in the smaller scale, note to note, singing one tone, imagining the next, feeling the change (propagation) before moving on and repeating the cycle. Diligent mindfulness and consistent effort over much time will lead you to the point where simply intending to sing will generate a response throughout your body and consciousness. You will be seeing/feeling your instrument, a master of your voice with all the range and colors of your art being your choice, rather than the limit of your ability. Oh happy day!

For a brilliant and wonderfully effective concept on the idea of a moving energy in the mouth, take a close look at pages 149-152 in E. Herbert-Caesari's The Alchemy of Voice, published in 1965 by Robert Hale, Limited, but currently out of print. It can be found in university libraries if not in search services/dealers like ABE Books. As with all five of Herbert-Caesari's titles, it contains comprehensive wisdom and truth most rare. On those pages there is a description of spinning wheels; a large wheel in the mouth and a smaller wheel above it. When imagined with awareness behind, they should spin with the speed of the frequency and the width of the tone column. For a very low note the speed would be slower and the width, maybe ⅜", narrowing as the pitch rises and smoothly moving onto the higher, smaller wheel for much greater speed and razor-thin width. The tone column tops find their rightful places automatically and the vowel thoughts are imagined on the outer rims when you get the hang of this. Any image that helps eliminate the temptation to "place" a note or feeling is a friend of mine. I draw them in Figure 15 as I feel them.

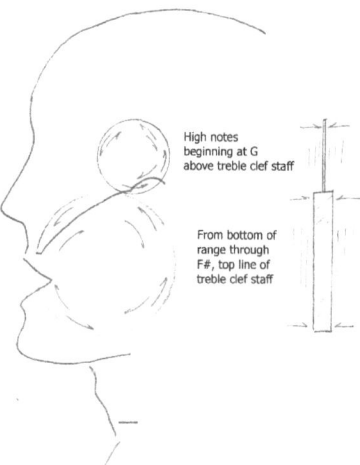

Fig. 15 Tone wheels that spin in sync with pitch frequency and narrow in sync with the tone columns, reflecting the vocal cords' opening. "See" the narrowing edges of the wheels from behind. Vowels ride tangentially on the rims of the speeding wheels.

Three important elements to this image: 1) A backward motion of the wheels (clockwise in the view in Fig. 15) helps to affect a lift of the soft and hard palates more than a forward motion (counterclockwise in Fig. 15). 2) When the spinning energy transfers to the upper wheel, you must continue to sense spatially the lower wheel. The image of the wheels lends structural sensation, while the sense of their spinning promotes proper function. 3) When you mentally place vowels tangentially on the wheels, you must imagine that they offer no resistance to the spin.

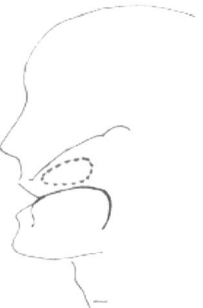

Fig. 16 Egg-shaped expansive energy, with constantly expanding motion in sync with the sound beam momentum.

One can also imagine a full-body expansive momentum, a feeling that begins before the first note and ends after the last note has sounded. Mentally generated and subtly perceived in the physical, it helps to maintain the flow of your sound and the brace of the singing body. This is also an advanced concept, more easily understood after a minimum constant breath pressure has been realized throughout your range and you have a very clear vision of the yawn energies at work.

In figure 16, I have indicated an egg-shaped energy in the mouth. Open to the pre-yawn state for the word, "huNG," think "a" as in bat, then "u" as in "root." Now imagine a vibrant egg-shaped energy on its side with the larger end toward the back of the mouth. Imagine the "egg" in a constant state of expansion in minute, oil-smooth increments and sync it with the energy of the sound beam. The "egg" never contracts and YOU MUST NOT INTENTIONALLY EXPAND YOUR MOUTH OPENING. Simply imagine the expansion of the "egg" and take note of the responses in your ribcage, pelvic diaphragm, lower jaw, hard palate, anywhere and everywhere. This imagined action will lend considerable elegance to your singing.

The most fun begins when your vocal body is structurally functional and musically responsive to your concept of the style; in other words, when it is built to the balance, flexibility and strength I mention so often. At that point you can imagine these three centers of momentum in Figure 17 spinning like turbines in sync with the pitches of your music, responding in speed and size. Along with the downward energy into the tailbone of the long arc, it helps to keep you grounded and to generate an even presence of breath in that all-so-important minimal pressure that you want against the underside of the vocal cords.

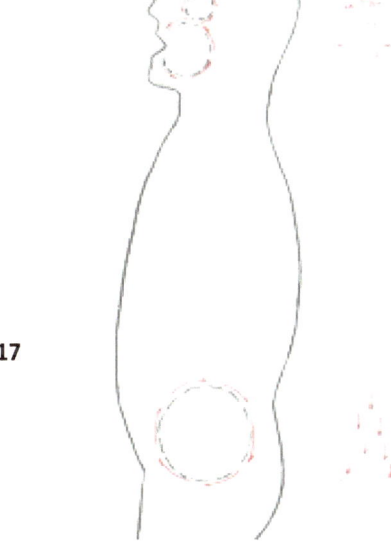

Fig. 17

The three "wheels of momentum" spin in sync with one another as well. Your image of them alone, shown here in side view and mind's-eye appearance, creates the effect of their action. Even with your mouth closed, sitting in a chair, the very thought of them spinning at "idle," no pitch conceived, creates a response throughout your body. The response of speed and size in the wheels then changes in sync with thoughts of melody. This is imagined but the feelings and effects are immediately evident in an oil-smooth legato and greatly increased breath control.

Spinning in sync with the frequency of the pitch, the mouth wheel narrows as the pitch rises until it is the same width as the upper, smaller wheel. At that point the energy of tone slides up to the higher wheel, which continues to spin and diminish in width in sync with the frequencies. The mouth wheels can spin in your imagination in either direction according to your comfort. I prefer a clockwise spin as viewed from the right side of my head. The vowel thought is placed tangentially on the wheel's edge, never pressed to the wheel, never offering resistance to the wheel's spinning action. This image creates a path for the tonal columns to your highest notes quite naturally.

The widest wheel, like a sphere, under your pelvic diaphragm at the base of your torso spins in sync with the pitch frequencies. Please look carefully at the illustration and notice that the pelvic wheel should always spin backward, clockwise, observed from the left side. It does not need to narrow with greater speed but must remain free of resistance as well as the upper wheels. Its presence and action cause the pelvic diaphragm to dome, giving a sense of lift to the torso and allowing the thoracic diaphragm to dome and maintain breath presence against the underside of the vocal cords.

> **WHEN THE SINGER'S AWARENESS ENCOMPASSES ALL THREE WHEELS SIMULTANEOUSLY, A LEVEL OF POISE AND BOUYANCY IS ATTAINED THAT IS A KEY TO MASTERY.**

IN SUMMARY

Discussing the singing body, it is important to know that I present the elements of a fully balanced and coordinated vocal instrument capable of great singing at the highest level. That level includes Enrico Caruso on one hand and Frank Sinatra on another; Rosa Ponselle and Ella Fitzgerald. The style is a product of your imagination's ability to conceive the expected tone and phrasing; the instrument responds to your imagination. There are so many beautiful voices but so little great singing today.

The development of the physical instrument is this simple: 1) The vocal cords must be stretched to maximum length, which necessarily thins and tightens them to a tensile strength capable of responding to changing the opening of the cords that is required for a specific frequency or pitch. 2) The mouth in its entirety, from front teeth to pharynx must be free to accept and reflect what amounts to columns or vortices of excited air created by the opening and closing of the vocal cords. 3) The torso must be poised (balanced readiness) in an elastic expansion, governed by your thoughts of tone and phrasing and responsive to the melodic line as though you were speaking to various distances. What do I mean by that? If someone were standing next to you, your voice would be modulated to that distance. If the person were 30 or 100 or 300 feet away your modulation would automatically be adjusted so that the listener might hear you. You would not consciously expand, contract, push or pull this, that or another part of your body to be heard. This is partially what I mean when I say that you play the vocal instrument with your imagination. Keep your mind constantly focused when you practice and perform.

I was listening to a classical music radio station while driving recently. Following the brilliant trumpeter, Håken Hardenberger's playing of a concerto, the announcer quoted him as saying (my paraphrase): 'the secret to playing the trumpet is like walking a dog; you have to walk the dog, not let the dog walk you. You do not play the trumpet with your breath; you play it with your mind.' Talk about validation. Awareness of what our consciousness is, how it works and how we can use it to affect any change in our lives is not new, and is growing exponentially and globally. I am just presenting here how I see it relating to expressive, communicative singing. Spend some minutes daily with the contemplations to exercise your mind's eye and your mind's ear, hearing within as though wearing earphones, which happens when you are seeing from within through, not with your eyes.

What could be simpler or more complex? The good news is that, given guidance to understand what the flexible, physical instrument feels like, we can learn how it functions by observing our body's responses to thoughts of pitch and vowel, thereby creating habits of coordination in obedience to nature. Imposing what we perceive to be the physical functions of singing, like intentional drawing in or pushing out of abdominal muscles, holding ourselves somehow in the name of posture or relaxing any part of ourselves confounds easy and accurate musical vocal expression. We are vibration, music is vibration and vibration is only optimal in the absence of inhibition. Intentional physical effort inhibits nature's way.

Use the physical tools presented throughout this book to engage the proper coordination, observe the response in the body and, by repetition, create muscle memories, physiology that is engaged at the thought of singing.

Put another way, as with all things body-mind oriented, if you can find an image that engenders a physical response, which speaks to the optimal function of your vocal body, rather than a direct physical attempt to meet a coordinative need, you are on your way to seemingly effortless emission of the sound you desire. What comes first, the feeling in response to thought or the image describing the feeling? Does the image engender the feeling or the feeling, the image? Whichever seems to happen first in the growing stages, the very thought of singing, even with your mouth closed, establishes the sense of yourself as an instrument, which draws the vocal body into position for accurate function once the instrument is understood and completely balanced. Now breathe.

APPENDICES

Appendix A
A CONTEMPLATION

SIT UPRIGHT WITH YOUR *EYES closed* in a straight-backed chair or, if you can, in a yoga lotus position. Imagine that your head is hollow as though inflated, there being a sense of energy present inside urging outward at every point and giving constancy to the shape of your hollow head. **Always maintain the hollow or inflated feeling.** Now imagine a vertical line from the top center of your head descending the length of your torso. Got that? Call it a "Y" axis. Now imagine a line crossing it at 90^0 about an inch above and toward the back of the ears. Think of it as an "X" axis and their intersection as 0,0. See these axes in the center of your head near the top of the "wall" (see Fig. 8, p. 40).

Your awareness is behind so there is space between it and the 0,0 point. There is also space between that point and the front of your skull and, obviously, on either side, to the left and right, as well as above it to the top of your skull and below to your pelvic diaphragm. You don't have to search for this image. Seeing it with your mind's eye, suspended in the upper-middle of your "hollow" head is enough to create it.

Place a small apple on the "crosshairs" of the axes just described, then a carrot, then a candle whose flame covers the intersection. See them clearly? All this is your mind's eye, your imagination, at work. Another test of its presence in your awareness is to look carefully at the room where you sit in a 360° arc. Take your time, then close your eyes and try to see everything you noticed when your eyes were open. The more you do this the more you will remember.

Contemplate that 0,0 point with eyes open or closed. Mentally place a vowel gently on 0,0 and keep it present there, not pressing, but by mentally repeating it, as though riding a beam of sound energy. Mentally repeating a vowel while sustaining a note or thinking ahead when singing a phrase is an important technique to help maintain your mind in a creating state where there is no tension. Place another vowel there in the same manner, then another and so on through a string of vowels. Notice the subtle physical movements with each vowel placement? Open your mouth as though to yawn, with lips neutral, and place a, e, i, o, u sequentially on the point 0,0. I refer always to the Italian "a" as in "ah," open "e" as in "get," "i" as in "ee," closed "o" as in "oh" and "u" as in "boot."

Observe the movements in your pharynx (if you wonder where your pharynx lies, it is the upper back of your mouth, essentially between your ears). Remember that if you attempt to affect those movements physically you will create tension that you don't want. Eyes still closed, mouth open as though yawning, lips and facial flesh neutral and unmoving (not held, just willed calm), repeat this for many minutes at a time and as often as you like. These sensations are some of your best friends. Take time to notice muscular reaction/movement even in your pelvic area as you do this.

In the following casual sketch of a contemplative state of mind, behind and left views, the relative sense of the 0,0 point described above is shown as a red dot.

Fig. 18

Appendix B
HAND JIVE FOR SINGERS

JUST AS THE PHYSICAL BODY can respond to particular mental images with accurate movements and energies, so too can external physical metaphors/movements generate subtle actions in the physical vocal body, which help to develop desired habits of coordination.

Certain gestures reinforce your senses of vocal body structure; others of the momentum and rhythm of breathing; the actions of the pelvic diaphragm; movements within the mouth/pharynx; and still others of the ever-changing sensations of resonance.

A DVD is planned for release in 2017 explaining and demonstrating the when, why and how of the 26 exercises. Here I present three of the most important gestures as photos. Remember that all parts of you, from the brace of your elastic muscular shell to the smallest detail of your mouth/pharynx, are in a constant state of flux when you sing. The only thing that you "hold" is your breath as though you were swimming under water.

"Raising the Roof"

This movement has the effect of maximizing the lift of the palatal arch throughout the exercise or phrase while not actually holding anything up. It should begin with the thought of what's coming before you inhale/replenish and continue into the silence beyond the last tone. Go slowly and steadily, not quickly, not far.

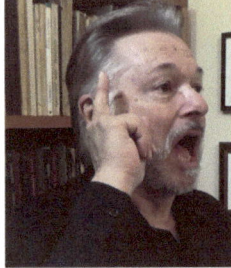  

"Gathering Energy"

Properly engaging the action of the pelvic diaphragm while breathing and singing is frequently misunderstood and cannot be overrated. This simple movement of the hands as though compressing a sponge or ball of energy without any strain, helps you to feel the engagement and function of the pelvic diaphragm during breath replenishment **and** singing. You understand that engagement by observing, not by trying to effect it. Make no direct muscular effort in your abdomen, but rather bring your hands together no closer than shown and notice the response around the pelvis; to me as though a grapefruit-sized sphere gives lift to the pelvic diaphragm (Fig. 17). Its spinning in your imagination helps to prevent tension.

"Off the Ski Jump"

Never performed below the level of the cheek bones, this rapid movement lifting up at the extension, imitating the flight off a ski jump, should be enjoyed when singing arpeggios as in exercise 4 (see "26 Exercises for the Voice") ahead. It is also important at the end of any phrase as a release which helps to maintain the singing position. When you are familiar with its feelings, you can imagine doing the movements with considerable positive effect. It should be rapid but not violent. To better feel the inception of a note you can alternate breath-tone, breath-tone with an extension movement for each.

Appendix C
FREQUENTLY ASKED QUESTIONS

What's the best posture for singing?

In a state of poise, balanced readiness, whether erect, sitting or even lying down. I am reminded of a performance of "Tosca" at the Met in which, after being thrown to the floor by Scarpia, Maria Callas remained on her back to sing "Vissi d'arte" and electrified an already-adoring audience. Your carriage must be a result of thought, not of holding yourself this way or that. Can you imagine that Callas, on that extraordinary night, allowed herself to go limp and "relax"? Singing is an electric mind-body expression: the current of that electricity dependent upon the emotion of the moment. Ask yourself silently, "How long is my spine?" Then: "Is my skull balanced on my spine?" That will go a long way to helping you feel poise when standing.

How do I relax my jaw?

Relaxation is important in the dentist's chair and in hypnosis, but in functioning as a singing instrument, you want to achieve *poise,* a state of balanced readiness. Learn how the jaw actually moves, what exercises strengthen and make fluid that movement, and you will find tension-free function, which seems to be relaxation but is actually balanced, poised coordination.

How can I get the sound out of my nose?

I could tell you why the sound is in your nose, but it's better to feel a way of singing that eliminates the problem without drawing attention to the cause(s). The age-old way is to sing a tone or phrase holding your nostrils closed. If it's in your nose you will know it. An effective way for many is to **imagine** inhaling to the top back of your skull **while singing.** That will lift the soft palate, whose laziness is a possible cause of the nasal tone. Smoothly transitioning from "NG" to a pure vowel also has the effect of lifting the soft palate. You can enjoy nasal resonance without nasality.

How do I support high notes?

There is no altitude or depth to notes. Those who don't understand that can be seen stretching their necks upward to "reach" or worse, to "hit" a high note. What is high or low is the number, the frequency of a pitch, like A-220 or the octave above that: A-440. Taking the octave as example, 220 refers to the cycles of sound waves per second. If in the same second you want to admit 440 cycles, each wavelength or cycle must be half the size as that of the lower octave while moving at twice the velocity. If you conceive notes as existing in a beam whose inner core varies in speed and size according to the pitch, you will avoid the reaching. The momentum, mentally conceived, is forward and constant.

The body should brace to sustain a pitch in *response to the thought* of that pitch, not because of intentional muscular pressure. If you want to call to someone across the street, you don't consciously beef up your chest and abdominal muscles and try to push the sound out. You imagine his or her ability to hear you and call out; just let go. Imagination has asked your body for the proper brace. When singing, once the response mechanisms of the entire body are balanced and strengthened, the thought of a note is enough to engage all parts for its successful emission.

How do I know the right amount of breath to support my tone?

Your ego, your conscious mind, doesn't know, but your imagination does. You only need one breath pressure. There must be what I have learned to call an indispensable minimum of air pressure present against the underside of the vocal cords after inhalation. You must learn to close (approximate, adduct) and keep closed the vocal cords at the end of inhalation. From that moment on, the thought of pitch adjusts the vocal cords, which in turn demands a concomitant brace of the body. Please don't fall into the trap of believing that you can consciously apply the correct "muscle" to your larynx/torso/diaphragm for a given pitch. Many physical elements coordinate to adjust the vocal cords and allow a sustained vocal tone, but they are all best governed by thought.

Is breathing the same for men and women?

The only physical difference between men and women in the entire singing process is during inhalation. As I have said, the most efficient and tension-free manner of breathing is to allow the breath through the nose and/or mouth while mentally singing the next note(s). By nose, I refer to the opening in the skull before the flesh and cartilage that sits up front (Figure 13 on page 63). DO NOT breathe through the nostrils, as that produces tension.

That's true for all.

Now that said, women instinctively inhale in one smooth motion as though inflating a bell, which is their ribcage. Men, however, inhale in two consecutive actions: the first, a bell-like inflation of the ribcage; the second, a rising and general expansion of the upper chest.

What role does the diaphragm play in singing?

The thoracic diaphragm, situated between the bottom of your sternum and your spine, is the agent of consistent breath pressure against the underside of the vocal cords. Confusion and tension result when direct control of the thoracic diaphragm is attempted. It must be released into its natural domed form to maintain the minimum breath pressure necessary for tone production. This release occurs when, rather than breathing deeply and down to the diaphragm or abdomen, you think of the breath as energy and draw that energy into your vocal body simultaneously through the nose and/or mouth and from below the pelvic diaphragm. Conceiving that energy as a spinning sphere, the effect is to lift the pelvic diaphragm into a dome that functions in tandem with the thoracic diaphragm and the soft palate supplying all the "support" the tone needs.

Of course you replenish actual air through the nose and mouth, but a valid and worthwhile perception is that the breath descends to the pelvis where it meets an upward-flowing and spinning energy with resistance equal to that upward flow and spin. Lilli Lehmann describes what the Germans call "Atemstauen," breath-block (op. cit., p. 23), opposing energies with equal force at the solar plexus. I see that happening at the crest of the dome of the pelvic diaphragm as well, a concept that nearly eliminates the dangers of tightening the thoracic diaphragm, a possibility against which Lehmann warned. It must all begin mentally. Let breath happen. See yourself from within, inflated head-to-hips. Use the images prescribed here and let the diaphragms function as nature designed them. The adjustments of the vocal cords allow tones with sustained minimal air pressure, not adjusted air pressure.

How do I sing over the passaggio and the breaks between my registers?

When you study yourself as a singing instrument as I prescribe in this book, you will learn the adjustments from each half-step to the next, up or down. Then you will understand that each pitch in your range is a passage, an all-body adjustment to the next. There will not be plateau-like leaps from one note to another, no passaggio, no bug-a-boo F# or Eb...nothing to fear, thanks to information leading to the experience of feeling, not listening.

This is an important question because it speaks to fundamental flaws rampant in vocal teaching. When you trust your physical response to thought to show you how this natural action happens, your self-esteem shoots through the roof, your confidence soars, and your voice is yours to enjoy.

How can I tell where I am tight?

If there is tension anywhere, there will soon be tension everywhere. Inflation and/or "softening" can help to reduce it.

For example, if you catch your eyes staring intently, soften them. If you are seeing with your mind's eye from within, your external eyes will already be soft. If your legs are tight, inflate your knees or ankles or hips. You can think this for any part of yourself.

A major manifestation of tension can occur in the upper back and neck. Inflate the tops of your trapezius muscles between your shoulders and inflate your neck as though wearing a whiplash brace. At times inflate the back of your skull, the occipital lobes and neck muscles which insert into them. Inflate the orbits of your eyes or mouth. Inflate your ears. Pick an area, inflate it and observe what happens everywhere.

How can I improve the sound of my voice?

By learning the feelings of resonance. Maximum resonance is a product of uninhibited vibration and that vibration is only possible in an environment of freedom. Learn the feeling of freedom and your resonance will improve.

What are the best exercises to warm up?

Warming up is really tuning the voice like any instrument for optimum performance. I like to refer my students to a checklist:
- Is your mind in the game, your awareness above and behind?
- Remind yourself that notes are not high or low. Frequencies are higher or lower numbers and they are just denoting speed and implying size.
- Study the feelings of change and movement when you

THINK of various vowels while in a yawn-like expansiveness.
- Study the feelings of change and movement when you THINK of various pitches with the yawn senses.
- Begin with exercises which help your body understand a single breath pressure throughout your range, like exercises 1 and 2 of those included in this book.
- Next, add exercises which help you feel and see the flexible and balanced structure of the head/mouth/pharynx, like scales on the ng of "hung," opening to a vowel.

What should I eat and when before singing?

Questions about when to eat before singing, what to eat, how much and with what effect on breathing are answered by individual needs. We now know enough about diet to understand that complex carbohydrates are more energy-producing in the long run than simple sugars. Animal protein frequently requires more energy to digest than it supplies for action. You want the energy from the food, while not feeling "full."

One of the most energy-yielding meals I prepare is a bowl of either escarole, kale or broccoli rabe (organic, if possible), sautéed in garlic and EV olive oil with flakes of red pepper. With a slice or two of simple bread (the ingredients list doesn't read like a chemist's shopping list) and three hours for digestion, I am fit as a fiddle...there we are back to being an instrument. If you are singing or will be interacting with other people, you might want to use a mouthwash after brushing. In general, a good habit is to: Leave the cannoli. Take the broccoli.

Appendix D
SEVEN PILLARS OF VOCAL WISDOM

KNOW THAT SELF-AWARENESS DISPELS SELF-CONSCIOUSNESS

OBSERVE YOURSELF FROM SLIGHTLY ABOVE AND BEHIND, LOOKING NOT WITH YOUR EYES BUT THROUGH THEM.

FEEL YOURSELF AS THE INSTRUMENT OF SINGING AND CARE FOR THAT INSTRUMENT AS THOUGH IT WERE UNIQUE, FOR IT IS.

ALWAYS THINK AHEAD KNOWING THAT APPROPRIATE, ACCURATE PHYSICAL ACTION RESULTS FROM THOUGHT.

KNOW THAT YOUR BODY IS THE VEHICLE FOR YOUR SOUND, NOT THE CREATOR. YOUR IMAGINATION IS THE CREATOR.

BE MINDFUL, BE PATIENT AND PERSEVERE AS YOU BUILD THE RESPONSIVE VOCAL BODY.

WHEN YOU PERFORM, COMMUNICATE. ALLOW YOUR INTENTION TO DEMAND OF YOUR VOICE WHATEVER IS REQUIRED TO THAT END.

Appendix E

26 EXERCISES

Compiled by Franco Spoto
As a Workbook Companion to

THINK FEEL SING
A CLEAR PATH TO EASY SINGING

ABOUT THE EXERCISES

GENERAL CONSIDERATIONS:

While the exercises are not presented in any particular order, numbers 1 and/or 2 should begin your daily work. The others are here to choose as you build your awareness and familiarity of the instrumental you. Number 18, which helps to connect body and breath, works well before 1 and 2 are attempted.

At the start and for an indefinite time, BEGIN EVERY EXERCISE with the thought of "huNG", opening to the ng sound into what is called the open-mouthed hum. To be sure that you are experiencing the maximum vertical stretch within your head, place an index finger beside and in front of one ear and move it slowly upward. What does that feel like? Then maintaining that feeling, think the sound a, as in bat, and notice what happens on the entire front quadrant of your head, from your upper teeth. Maintaining that too, now think of u, as in toot, and notice what you feel high in the head behind the vertical. Notice what moves and how. That is the structure within which all of nature's mechanics can function; your physical instrument. That structure is never static and must never collapse or all other functions will suffer along with your sound.

When singing the open-mouth hum employing the word, hung, and dwelling on the ng, begin it elegantly with a gentle "h", followed by a clear "uh" vowel, then opening to the ng rather than biting down on it.

Sing slowly at first, remembering to maintain the hollow inflated feeling from head to hips and the image of long arc from the upper back of your skull to your tail bone (coccyx). Your sense of inflated hollowness should encompass 360 degrees and never diminish. With your awareness behind and above you, the instrument, you will see out through your eyes, not with them. The longer you contemplate this awareness of your carriage, the sooner it will become a most helpful habit.

Vowel formation begins functionally in the pharynx with an image at the apex of the coming- together sensation you experience when thinking of "U" or any vowel during a yawn's expansion. To understand what that means for you, continually ask yourself "What does this feel like?" The answer should not be one word, but rather a clear description of what you feel, where you feel it, and how various parts are moving. The vowel image high in the pharynx is like a stencil on a light's lens. What you feel then in the mouth is the reflection of that light, as though the lens image were on a flashlight and the feeling in the mask on what seems like the upside of the hard palate, were the light on the wall. Here are vowel images which work well for me and my students. The image for a long "E" (as in meet) is one that I first saw somewhat differently designed in the works of E. Herbert-Caesari. Think the pure vowel and remain in a yawn-like ("hung") expansion while simply seeing the image "stencil" at the "U" apex. The result will be a properly shaped receptor for the tonal column without your trying to form anything physically. When you have this mastered you will be able to think pure vowels throughout your range, while stencil images diminish in size from Eb-F#, and all pitches above

F# are imagined through the image of an upside-down "U", which itself diminishes to nearly a dot on the highest notes.

VOWEL	"STENCIL" IMAGE	IMAGE ABOVE STAFF
EE	⊙	∩
EH	8	∩
AH	O	∩
OH	o	∩
OO	∩	∩
Ö	8	∩
Ü	8	∩

The front of your face including lips is just that. Your mouth begins with your teeth and includes your tongue, hard and soft palates and pharynx, which, when all is understood, feels like an expanding balloon between your ears.

The voiced consonants, M, N, L, R, V, W, Y and Z must be pitched at the same frequency as the vowel that follows. Simply hearing/feeling the note ahead will help this action.

The symbol V indicates a breath. The symbol ⌒ indicates a release of the note as though propelling it mentally up and forward, or, if it works for you, as though it soars off a ski jump. This helps to keep the vocal cords and your pharyngeal structure in the singing position.

It's a good idea to take 30-90 seconds of rest between exercises. Rest is an important activity.

Regarding repetition of the exercises, there is no set number for every student. Take stock of your concentration, of fatigue factors; diminishing returns being a source of frustration. Work within parameters of common sense until the desired feelings are "second nature"; 10 times, 100, 1,000? Who's counting? There is no failure; only result. Work mindfully until the desired result is seen, felt, enjoyed, focusing always on what you intend, not on what you don't want to do.

A word of caution: As you work toward building good habits, old habits will be strong. Your concentration must be keen during daily mindful exercise (that said, it can be helpful to rest your voice one day a week; a resting of the whole body). Soon, from lack of attention, the old habits will have atrophied while the new have gained strength. There will be a period of equal strength between the old and new, a no man's land of frustration when neither set of feelings/muscles is strong enough for consistency. Then the new feelings take firmer hold while the old continue to weaken and confidence builds rapidly into your singing. The fun begins.

THE GREAT SCALE:

Lilli Lehmann, in her landmark work, Meine Gesangkunst, How To Sing, first published in English by The Macmillan Company in November of 1902, devotes an entire chapter to what she calls "The Great Scale". I don't know if the term was her invention, but as a title and a description it has no equal, in my opinion. As you allow air into your lungs imagine that you are already singing the first pitch and vowel. Thinking ahead and mentally singing what's coming is the only sure way to "take" a tension-free and sufficient breath...always.

As you sing the first note of the scale, immediately rethink the vowel, which will allow the thoracic and pelvic diaphragms to dome, raise the soft palate in tandem with them and be the propagation form for the next note. When you hear/feel the next note, you will feel the changes in your mouth/pharynx particularly at the soft palate. That is the propagation of the next note, the release into a new state of poise, structure and flexibility. Take time to feel before allowing the next note to sound and so on up the scale through the fifth. Breathe, singing the fifth in your mind. Continue by singing the fifth again and repeating the process up the scale through to the octave. Breathe and return to the lower tonic. Sing this from bottom to top in your range. If there is time for only one exercise on a given day, this should be the one. Lehmann posits that students sing it twice a day, professionals once. I agree.

This exercise is a truth-builder for both men and women as we have the same muscles and coordinations. The difference between men and women as singers is in the inhalation where for women it is one continuous, bell-like inflation of the rib cage, and for men a two-fold action with the bell-like downward expansion followed by the upper chest.

THE BREATH EQUALIZER:

The Great Scale is a building, stabilizing, restorative tonic for all voices. This next scale helps the singer to understand the feelings of equal and minimal breath pressure. While singing only the lowest note with full voice at a comfortable dynamic, pay attention to what you feel everywhere as you hear/imagine the full melodic scale. Then sing the scale while imagining that you are only singing the first note. What does that feel like? The longer you look the more you will see/feel.

THE NINE NOTE MAJOR SCALE:

One of the most common tools for building the voice and subject to many variations, sing it on the ng of the word, "HuNG", the open-mouthed hum, for the greatest senses of structural adjustments and resonance, particularly the adducted cords image from Fig. 6. Sing it on any vowel, mindful of the where, what and how of resonance and of the internal structure taught to you by the feeling of "Hung".

MOMENTUM

By momentum, in this context, I refer to the energetic direction of your sense of sound. The perceived beam of sound should always be moving in a forward wave whose size (diameter) and speed are in direct proportion to the frequency of the pitch: the higher the frequency, the faster the beam and narrower the diameter.

WITHIN A FLEXIBLE STRUCTURE, THOUGHT CREATES FORM, ALLOWING FUNCTION.

26 Exercises for the Voice

Compiled by
Franco Spoto

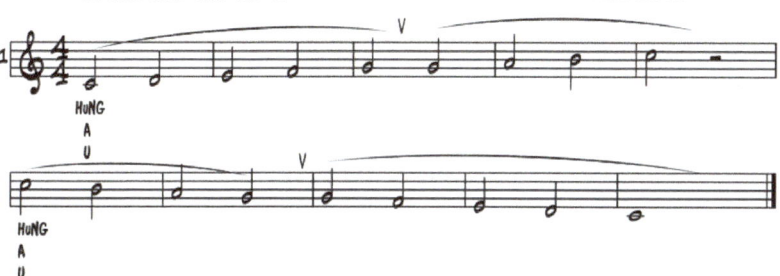

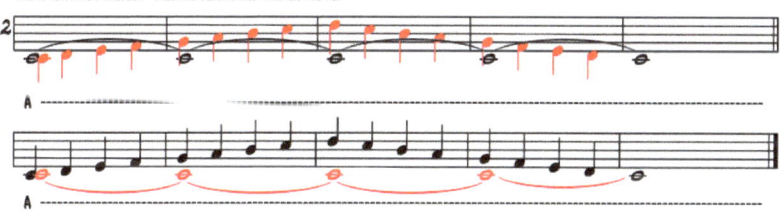

Singing: Nature's Gift To You | 119

GLOSSARY

7th CV or CERVICAL VERTEBRA: Lowest of the neck vertebrae and just above T1, the top of the back vertebrae, it is the prominent spinal bone felt between the shoulders.

CROWN OF THE STERNUM: The very top of the breast bone, connecting the left and right clavicles and feeling crescent-shaped to the touch.

HARD PALATE: The area of the roof of the mouth extending from the front teeth back to the palatal arch and uvula.

HYOID BONE: A u-shaped bone just under the tongue and above the larynx, sometimes called the tongue-bone.

LARYNX: The area atop the trachea containing the vocal cords with a complex of muscles, cartilage and ligaments.

MANDIBLE: the lower jaw or jaw-bone.

PHARYNX: Everything above the larynx, extending from the nasal cavities and including the upper back of the mouth, that part felt in extreme expansion during a yawn.

POSTERIOR FONTANELLE: The area of the skull where the left and right parietal bones meet the occipital bone, usually felt as the somewhat flat spot on the upper back of the skull.

SOFT PALATE: That very flexible area in the upper back of the mouth, behind the palatal arch where dangles the uvula.

UVULA: The soft hanging fleshy protuberance in the middle of the soft palate.

RECOMMENDED READING

WHILE ALL THESE ARE VERY valuable, the five Herbert-Caesari volumes should be studied, not just read, by anyone seriously interested in understanding singing mastery.

Herbert-Caesari, E., The Science and Sensations of Vocal Tone; London, J. M. Dent & Sons, 1936.

Herbert-Caesari, E., The Voice of the Mind; Boston, Crescendo Publishing Company, 1951.

Herbert-Caesari, E., Tradition and Gigli; London, Robert Hale Limited, 1958

Herbert-Caesari, E., The Alchemy of Voice; London, Robert Hale Limited, 1965

Herbert-Caesari, E., Vocal Truth, London, Robert Hale Limited, 1969

Lehmann, Lilli, How to Sing, New York, The Macmillan Company, 1944

Marafioti, Dr. P. Mario, MD, Caruso's Method of Voice Production, D. Appleton-Century Company, 1935

Frederick Husler and Yvonne Rodd-Marling, Singing: the Physical Nature of the Vocal Organ, New York, October House, 1965.

Todd, Mabel Ellsworth, <u>The Thinking Body</u>; New York, Dance Horizons, Inc.; unabridged 1937 edition.

Zemlin, Willard R., <u>Speech and Hearing Science</u>, Allyn & Bacon, 1998

Notes

[1] From <u>The Power of Awareness</u> by Neville. ©2010, Martino Publishing; ISBN: 1-57898-924-8.

[2] Robert Gibson as Frosch, the drunken jailer mocking Alfred, the Italian tenor singing offstage in a cell (played in that production by the author). Act 3 of Johann Strauss, Jr.'s <u>Die Fledermaus</u> at The Highfield Theater, Falmouth, MA, performed by The Oberlin College Gilbert and Sullivan Players.

[3] <u>Atlas of Human Anatomy</u>, Frank H Netter, M.D.;© Copyright 1989, CIBA-GEIGY Corporation

[4] <u>Speech and Hearing Science</u>, Willard R Zemlin, Copyright 1998, Allyn & Bacon

[5] e. e. cummings, <u>New Poems from Collected Poems</u> (1938) published by Harcourt, Brace & World, Inc. New York ISBN 0-15-172245-5

[6] Published by Princeton Book Company, ISBN: 9780871270146

[7] <u>Caruso's Method of Voice Production</u>, P. Mario Marafioti, M.D.; page 86 D. Appleton-Century Company, 1935.

[8] The Voice of the Mind, ©1951, 1963 by E. Herbert-Caesari; ISBN 87597-048-6, Crescendo Publishing Co.

[9] The edition I studied was issued in November 1944 with ©1930 by Richard Aldrich.

About the Author

IN HIS MID TEENS, FRANCO Spoto was fascinated with the sounds that a human voice could make. At first inspired by recordings of Mario Lanza, Enrico Caruso, Frank Sinatra and Tony Bennett, his fascination soon led to his own joy in singing and curiosity about the body as instrument for all voices. With formal education at the Oberlin College Conservatory of Music and The Juilliard School, his CV includes a faculty position at Bluffton University, solo engagements with Leonard Bernstein and Aaron Copland on the one hand and Sammy Cahn on the other. From a Broadway revival of The Most Happy Fella to Verdi's Requiem to Britten's Canticle III for Tenor, Horn and Piano to Schubert's Die Schöne Müllerin, Franco has been able to enjoy performing an unusually wide variety of musical styles. Currently, Franco lives in East Chatham, NY, teaching there and in New York City. Franco can be reached for comment or questions through his website: **www.mindyourvoice.com.**

www.ingramcontent.com/pod-product-compliance
Lightning Source LLC
Chambersburg PA
CBHW041724070526
44586CB00001B/2